SEX AND MARRIAGE

DATE DUE

1-30-92			

Demco, Inc. 38-293

**To My Mother and Father,
Married Fifty Years**

Imprimi Potest:
Stephen T. Palmer, C.SS.R.
Provincial, St. Louis Province
Redemptorist Fathers

Imprimatur:
+ Edward J. O'Donnell
Vicar General, Archdiocese of St. Louis

ISBN 0-89243-269-1
Library of Congress Catalog Card Number: 87-81195

Cover photo by Four By Five

Table of Contents

Introduction

Once upon a time it was enough to say about a confusing issue of faith or morals, "The Pope says." No more. So this little work will not pound on the pulpit (or the typewriter) to say what everyone probably knows already, "The Pope says." Many people just do not believe him. Or rather, they do not understand what he is saying in the name of the Catholic Church; honestly, he makes no sense to them.

But what the Catholic Church teaches through the pope and the bishops does make sense! Though readers may not come to agree with them, maybe they will come to the point of saying this, "I can see better where the bishops are coming from." These readers might also say, "The Catholic Church is not as confused about sexual morality as I had thought. She has a clear message. Even if I might not be ready to accept that message, she does make sense in what she says."

Maybe I can turn on a light or two for people who want to *understand*. And maybe I can make a plain fact even plainer: The Catholic Church is handing on a very clear sexual ethic to those who care to listen to Christ's appointed spokesmen — the bishops.

The question-and-answer format of this little book bears the accents of real people asking real questions. It also helps the

5

posing of sensitive questions that many people would like to ask of someone familiar with the moral wisdom of the Catholic Church. But this format also makes it harder to keep the material clearly organized. So let me give a quick view of the chapters for a better sense of direction.

The first chapter looks to Jesus Christ as the Church's sole authority. We see him address the issues of divorce and the connection of sexual morality with true religion. And we look at the Church trying hard to remain at the same time faithful to his teaching on divorce and gentle to his people.

Chapter two tries to illustrate how in the Catholic Church and her teaching we are confronted not by mere human opinion, but by the preaching of Jesus Christ. Yes, the preaching of Jesus Christ *in our day.*

Chapter three turns to the theme of sex as sacred. It says sex expresses a special promise, called a *covenant.*

Chapter four reflects on issues like homosexuality, contraception, and masturbation. It does this through a consideration of the human body as a house of worship, a temple of God. God has claimed us for his own, and we accept this claim by living moral lives.

Chapter five looks to the eternal life we are called to, which alone can make sense of the suffering so often involved in faithfulness to the moral teaching of Jesus Christ.

Finally, I hope that this point will be made sufficiently clear in the following pages: Chastity is not a matter of willpower. We cannot be chaste just by making up our minds to do so. We must seek chastity as a gift from God.

With Saint Augustine we can pray to God, "Command what you will, but give what you command." May the most pure Mother of God intercede for us.

John M. Hamrogue, C.SS.R.
Feast of St. Mary Magdalen
July 22, 1987

ONE

On Whose Authority?

Some Pharisees came up to him [Jesus] and said, to test him, "May a man divorce his wife for any reason whatever?" He replied, "Have you not read that at the beginning the Creator made them male and female and declared, 'For this reason a man shall leave his father and mother and cling to his wife, and the two shall become as one'? Thus they are no longer two but one flesh. Therefore, let no man separate what God has joined." They said to him, "Then why did Moses command divorce and the promulgation of a divorce decree?" "Because of your stubbornness Moses let you divorce your wives," he replied; "but at the beginning it was not that way. I now say to you, whoever divorces his wife (lewd conduct is a separate case) and marries another commits adultery, and the man who marries a divorced woman commits adultery."

His disciples said to him, "If that is the case between man and wife, it is better not to marry." He said, "Not everyone can accept this teaching, only those to whom it is given to do so. Some men are incapable of sexual activity from birth; some have been deliberately made so; and some there are who have freely renounced sex for the sake of God's reign. Let him accept this teaching who can" (Matthew 19:3-12).

Why is the Church so strict about divorce?

Because Jesus was! You can check out his words for yourself in the Gospels: Matthew 19:3-12 and Mark 10:2-12. Since each Gospel makes about the same points, let us stay with Saint Matthew. As he tells the story, a reader has to be struck by this, that Jesus' problems were the same as the Catholic Church's today as she tries to preach that marriage is forever. An audience asked Jesus about the rightness of divorce. How ugly to realize that the words in the question about the grounds of divorce — "for any reason whatever" — can mean either a serious or a trivial reason. Things had gotten so bad even then that some religious teachers were saying that a man might throw off his wife for any reason at all![1]

As Saint Matthew tells it, Jesus' questioners felt sure of themselves because they could even outdo our present-day appeal that "everybody does it." They knew that the most sacred lawgiver, Moses himself, had allowed divorce. What would Jesus reply to that?

Jesus replied that Moses allowed divorce because of the people's stubbornness, even though God had not originally planned on divorce: " . . . At the beginning it was not that way." If anyone would know that, Jesus would. He was there — at the beginning of everything! With his Father he had created the world, and knew what God had in mind and what he did not have in mind. His argument soars beyond law to the dreams God had for a world now gone so wrong. So in the Sermon on the Mount, too, which describes a new world in which the poor and persecuted are lucky, and the assailed seek no revenge but to pray for their tormentors, Jesus sternly forbids divorce.

And the disciples — his own friends and followers — are

8

shocked. They — we — are always shocked. In Matthew 19 they say that if this is how it is with a man and his wife, then why marry at all? So hard do they find his teaching! He then offers an alternative, renunciation of sex for the sake of this new world, the kingdom of heaven. The disciples had nothing to say about that idea! At any rate, Matthew does not recount anything else but leaves Jesus with the last stunning word: "Let him accept this teaching who can."

But even Jesus was a man of his own time, limited by it. And times have changed. Why can the Catholic Church not recognize that?

Have times really changed? People now as well as then find the yoke of marriage sometimes unbearable, and in this common experience think they fasten onto the incontestable last word. The Pharisees reminded Jesus that Moses allowed divorce. Surely everybody allows it, we say. As the saying goes: everything changes, nothing changes.

But let us spell it out more clearly. Not only does the Church face the same problem and the same opposition as Jesus did but she also carries the sublime burden of preaching in his name, on his authority. What she preaches she does not make up but has from him and his spirit. We will have more to say on this in the second chapter. But we ought to make this clear early on: The Church teaches as Jesus preaches. She stands on that fundamental authority.

Divorce speaks of the *end* of a marriage, of a tragic conclusion to what began so romantically and hopefully. Jesus, on the other hand, speaks in Matthew 19 of how it was "at the *beginning,*" when the earth was new. This is one reason that he is rejected: This world makes its rules on the basis of sad endings, while he looks to beginnings. And what beginnings! In clear reference to the Book of Genesis and its story of the first man and woman, he declares that the world ought now again be what God meant it to be from the beginning. His teaching transcends his time, which rejected it, and our time, which repeats the same rejection.

And his teaching is not just another law, either. We think, so often, that if the Catholic Church would just change its rules on this matter everything would be all right. Few Catholics truly appreciate that the Catholic faith is not built upon laws and rules, as important as these are. Hopefully, this little book will keep returning to this mystery. But for now let us envision Jesus, the Son of God, once present at the creation of the world, as he sets aside the law of the great Moses to help us see again what God had in mind for this world and what he means it to be once more. We must either concede that Jesus knew what he was talking about or that he was a fool.

As one who knew, he was speaking of *reality,* not of opinions or options.

Well, that is little help to me. I am not Adam or Eve, and I was not there at the beginning. I am here now and I am in a lot of trouble. What about me?

"What about me?" Priests like the present author have never felt the anguish and guilt of the failure of a marriage. But we have spoken to many people suffering this pain. And we have seen the tears of people not allowed to receive Communion because they live in a marriage the Church cannot recognize. What about them? Thank God, the Church has worked hard to find ways to deal with the tragic collapse of so many Catholic marriages. She grants so many more annulments, for one thing. That we can talk about later. For now, there is much more to the above question.

"I am not Adam or Eve, and I was not there at the beginning." But you *were* there at the beginning! That accounts for much of your pain here and now. In his authority and teaching, Jesus, in Matthew 19, appealed to the Book of Genesis not merely as a dry record but as the story written in the heart of anyone who has fallen in love and married. All of us can understand the theme of love songs: This never happened before! The singers also tell of destiny: It had to be this person, no one else. The Bible says that God wrote the story that way, having made them male and female and having so given them to each other that no one but God could ever separate them. So bride and groom, even in the face of divorces in their own families, with utter certitude promise to love each other till death parts them. And the rest of us gather to celebrate that man again has found woman and life will go on, will begin again.

What, then, is the Church supposed to do about that? What are the ballads to advise — that lovers give only part of their hearts, that they say "forever" while training for another job in case the marriage fails? If life and love ever came to that, human life would surely cease.

And what would the Church say to the young, to children? We priests have spoken to them, catechized them. They understand the romantic truth of the diamond industry's slogan: "Diamonds are forever." What does a diamond stand for? For love, they answer. And which is more real, love or diamonds? Love. How can anyone say that — since loving people die and diamonds last and last? Children do not know what to say to this. Still, out of their hearts they insist that love is more real than diamonds. What else would children think, or someone fumbling with an engagement ring while asking, "Will you marry me?"

Well, the Church watches out for those children and that young man and the young lady accepting the ring. If our first thought about the Church's attitude toward divorce is to say, "Too strict, rigid," we might think again. To see the Church as romantic is to gain a powerful insight into her sexual morality and her plight in an unromantic world.

I think I believe in romance. But I believe even more in happiness. I am frightened by the unhappiness I see in the

marriages of some of my friends and acquaintances. They are stuck. The Catholic Church seems to turn a deaf ear to people's pleas for happiness.

The Bible makes it clear that God intended marriage for the happiness of man and woman. Hear Adam's cry when he first saw Eve: "This one, at last, is bone of my bones and flesh of my flesh" (Genesis 2:23). Presumably, she felt the same way about him. The Church has long celebrated marriage as one great gift that humankind did not lose through original sin. Like all the guests at any wedding, she hopes and prays for the couple's happiness. How could she wish for anything else?

In the recent revision of her law, called *The Code of Canon Law,* the Catholic Church has been able to state her wish even more clearly than in the past. This law looks upon marriage as a covenant that seals "a partnership of the whole of life" (Canon 1055). By "whole of life" the Church does not refer to life only as computed in days and years, but to life as truly found in friendship, sharing, mutually knowing and being known, loving and being loved. So the Church sees this community of life as the heart and essence of marriage. In her law she sees the purpose of marriage to be the good of the couple and the procreation and upbringing of children. But what makes a marriage is the pledging of this communion and partnership.

Along the same lines, the former Code of Canon Law spoke of this pledge and this consent in terms of the body. One received and gave in marriage the right to the body for sexual intercourse open to conceiving a child. Had we understood that biblically, the older law would have been a far more powerful expression than the new law is. But we did not understand "body" as the Bible does. The Bible understands the body as the place and figure of the whole person; it sees one's body pretty much as one's whole self. The new Code of Canon Law does not use the word "body" in basically describing marriage, but clarifies its human and biblical

12

sense. In his joy at seeing Eve, Adam saw the gift of a whole person, a whole life. So does the Church see the gift of man and woman to each other in marriage.

Jesus would never be as strict as the Catholic Church! Other things are more important than worrying about whether people got married in church. I cannot believe he would worry about that.

Many people separate moral life from worship of God and from a personal relationship with him. Maybe you yourself scorn people who go to church every Sunday and say their prayers, only to spend much of the rest of their time clutching their money and criticizing other people. You would correctly judge their brand of religion to be a sham. The Bible sees things that way, too, and so did Jesus Christ.

In the fourth chapter of Saint John's Gospel, Jesus meets a woman coming to draw water at a well. The two of them get to talking about religion, though as a Samaritan she professed a different faith from Jesus'. She rejects the notion that God ought to be worshiped in Jerusalem; she and her countrymen have their own holy place, Mount Gerizim. In words that sound very modern to us, who are often annoyed by the conflicting claims of different Churches, Jesus tells her this:

"Yet an hour is coming, and is already here,

when authentic worshipers

will worship the Father in Spirit and truth" (John 4:23).

The religion he would bring would not be a narrow, "churchy" faith.

Yet, just before this, Jesus had interrupted a discussion on flowing, living water, which stands for a deep life with God. She began to thirst for this water. But Jesus brought her up short with a sudden remark: "Go, call your husband, and then come back here" (John 4:16). You see, Jesus knew she had been married five times and, after all, had merely moved in with her latest boyfriend. That mattered to him because it got in the way of the life he wanted her to enjoy and the worship he wanted her to give!

In Jesus' view — and the view of the whole Bible — moral living is a part of worship of God. In the Book of Exodus, God called the Jewish people, our forebears, out of Egypt. Moses asked God what he was to tell Pharaoh, who did not want to let go of a slave labor force. Tell them the Lord wants them to go out to the desert to celebrate with him, to offer him worship! Maybe religion annoys you because its purpose sometimes seems to be to make people lead neater and more tidy lives, to help parents raise respectful children, to organize a citizenry that supports a Church and salutes the flag. Clergymen can be such busybodies! But Jesus insists that he came to have people *worship God* in Spirit and in truth.

So worship is the heart of the matter. Yet, immorality erodes that heart, as it had debased the Samaritan woman. Consider the prophets of the Old Testament. Through them God protested that the worship of his people stank in his nostrils because they lived such grasping and unjust lives and because they worshiped sex and success like their pagan neighbors. He took this so seriously that he allowed pagan enemies to destroy his own temple at Jerusalem! He would have no worship but true worship, as Jesus will have no worship but that in Spirit and in truth. (Chapter four of this book takes up again this connection of worship with morality.)

An important part of the truth for the woman lay in the way she was living. She had to confess to that, and she did. How happily she announced Jesus' coming to her neighbors: ''Come and see someone who told me everything I ever did!'' (John 4:29)

But our age has some different ideas and dogmas about religion. Any priest would recognize the truth of this comment by two skilled observers of the religious scene:

> The majority of our reports indicate that many Americans belong to the ''not quite Christian'' category: They believe,

14

but without strong convictions. They want the fruits or reward of faith, but seem to dodge the responsibilities and obligations. They say that they are Christian but often without a visible connection to a congregation or religious worship.[2]

Where do people get ideas like that? How do they come to believe that laws of worship and moral living do not matter to God? They cannot have learned this from the Bible or from Jesus Christ.

We all love the story in John's Gospel (8:1-11) of the woman caught in adultery. The vigilantes dragged her before Jesus. Would he agree she should be stoned to death, as the sacred law prescribed? "Let the man among you who has no sin be the first to cast a stone at her." He then dawdled a while, scribbling something in the sand, as the accusers slipped away. Had anyone remained to condemn her? No, she noticed no one had. Jesus would not condemn her either. But he added this: "You may go. But from now on, avoid this sin." Somehow, Jesus' preaching gets trivialized. The Scripture here notes how seriously he took her sin. Yet somehow his last words of warning seem deleted and replaced by something like, "Have a nice day." Jesus deserves better than that. And his view of religion deserves better than that.

My wife tells me I do not care about her. But I work hard. I am faithful to her. What does she want?

Probably any priest would be a rich man if he had a dollar for every time he heard a complaint like your wife's. The priest will often hear it this way: "He is a good man. He supports the kids and me. But there is no affection, understanding. He does not want to talk about things. I guess he feels he gives me everything when he comes home with his pay. But I am miserable." Sometimes, however, the husband is *not* a good man at all. He may even be cruel.

You sound like a good man. You ask what your wife wants. Ask her. She may not be able to speak very clearly about what she wants; but listen carefully. Most likely she will be trying to tell you that she wants *you,* that is, your time, your presence, your attention, your tenderness. If so, she will be asking for what she has a right to in marriage: a sharing of lives. Maybe she will be asking for too much. Then you might help her to understand that.

Take her seriously. She may feel more desperate than you think. And look to your own sense of obligation in your marriage. If you think that you have done everything for the week when you have brought home the bacon, then your wife may have grounds not just for a divorce. She may have grounds for an annulment of your marriage by the Catholic Church.

What is an annulment?

An annulment is a judgment by the Church, in her own court system, that a real marriage never took place, that it is "null" from the beginning. A divorce, on the other hand, ends a marriage without consideration whether or not it was truly a marriage from the first. Catholic dioceses have courts to handle annulment cases. Anyone who needs to or ought to look into an annulment can see a parish priest.

Until fairly recent years, very few annulments were granted. Now we often hear of them. Theologically, two factors help account for this: first, the emphasis of the Second Vatican Council on marriage as a covenant, that is, a solemn personal relationship; second, the impact of the behavioral sciences, psychology especially, on the Church's practice.[3] Pastorally and practically there is a third reason: Many Catholics have suffered through divorces and have entered second marriages; they now are seeking ways to reconcile themselves to the Church.

Not too long ago, then, we would sometimes hear of the annulment of a marriage because the couple were incapable of physically consummating it. Personal incompatibility, we knew, stood up as grounds for divorce in a civil court, but it was not usually considered in an annulment. So much of this has changed. The Church now emphasizes much more than in the past that marriage is to be a loving, personal relationship. A marriage that never could amount to that is no marriage at all in her eyes. And she does not restrict the evidence of nullity in such a marriage to sexual inability.

Sometimes no one would quarrel with the Church's practice. Imagine two people married in church at the age of eighteen. Because the girl was pregnant, both parents urged them to marry. Within a year they had broken up. Everyone would say, "Why, that was no marriage at all."

No, I would not quarrel with that one. But a pillar of our parish recently divorced his wife of twenty-six years, received an annulment, and married his secretary. To me, that is a divorce.

What can we say? Some annulments are very hard to understand. We should never pry into even the most confusing of them. A sacred privacy and secrecy surrounds the proceedings of an annulment. It is not at all like a divorce, often a battle open to the public. And very often the evidence favoring an annulment is psychological; experts decide upon it.

Yet we priests have often heard people tell us privately, "Father, everyone thinks we have a model marriage. If only they knew!" So much is kept hidden from the neighbors, even from the family. And the highest of the Church's marriage courts, the Roman Rota, is willing to consider marriage cases in which the spouses generally get along with people but seem peculiarly unable to get along with *each other!*[4]

A friend of mine is married outside the Church. I notice she is receiving Communion again. I guess she noticed I looked

puzzled. No, she told me, no annulment. But a priest assured her she could receive Communion again. Do I still look puzzled?

Yes, you do, and probably there is nothing for it, either, except to respect your friend's conscience and the confidentiality of her relationship to her priest.

No priest can annul a marriage secretly, on his own. But in what is called "the internal forum" he can advise people on the level of their conscience. An annulment works in the external forum; it involves testimony and records that at least a few people are allowed to see, and a declaration of nullity that is an official and public document. But a priest working in the internal forum keeps no records and divulges no secrets. When he hears confessions, he is working in the internal forum. No one can ask him about this work and he cannot talk about it. He must keep the secrets of another person's conscience.

So even if your friend would discuss the matter with you, you will never hear the priest's side of the conversation. Your friend might tell you, "He told me to go ahead and receive Communion." Maybe he did. But maybe he would be surprised to hear himself quoted in those words.

At any rate, be calm and be kind — peaceful, not puzzled. Take it for granted that your friend is somehow all right with God and the Church.

Footnotes

1. *The Jerome Biblical Commentary* (Englewood Cliffs: Prentice-Hall, 1968), 43:131.
2. George Gallup, Jr., and David Poling, *The Search for America's Faith* (Nashville: Abingdon, 1980), p. 42.
3. Lawrence G. Wrenn, *Annulments,* 4th ed. revised (Washington, D.C.: Canon Law Society of America, 1983), p. 3.
4. *Ibid.,* p. 40.

TWO

What Does the Church
Know About Sex?

To those not married and to widows I have this to say: It
would be well if they remain as they are, even as I do myself;
but if they cannot exercise self-control, they should marry. It
is better to marry than to be on fire. To those now married,
however, I give this command (though it is not mine; it is the
Lord's): a wife must not separate from her husband. If she
does separate, she must either remain single or become
reconciled to him again. Similarly, a husband must not
divorce his wife (1 Corinthians 7:8-11).

**So many serious experts have other things to say on love and
sex. Why should I listen to the Catholic Church?**

You raise the issue of *authority,* or the basis for believing or
taking seriously somebody's opinion or teaching. We worry about
our travel plans if the weatherman warns of a winter storm,
because he is the expert. We would worry about *him* if he rolled up

his weather charts and began a lesson on cooking or on moral life. We honor the experts; we defer to their authority in their own fields.

Who are the authorities whose word forms your approach to love, sex, and life? Maybe you have not thought about them much, but maybe you should. On their say-so, maybe more than you realize, you are building your life and your relationships. We priests meet more and more people who suffer anguish and puzzlement as their loves and marriages collapse on them. How can this be happening, they ask? They have been playing by the rules as they learned them. Trouble is, the rules have been laid out by soap operas, or by magazines like *Playboy* and *Cosmopolitan*. Some experts write a second book that announces that the approach of their first one had it all wrong. But this second book can be trusted! Some experts may have little or no moral authority at all. It might be a good idea for you to do an inventory of your experts, the ones whose word you live by.

Are you saying the Church is an expert? She seems to have learned very little about sex in two thousand years. She is so far behind the times!

Up-to-dateness sells newspapers, which print the date at the top of the page like a claim to authority, as indeed it is. But what a difference a day makes! After one day we use the paper to wrap fish heads for the garbage. The Church has never worried too much about being up-to-date. Perhaps she should have. But it is one thing to say she is behind the times, when more likely the trouble for us newcomers is all the time she has behind her. Whatever someone might have to say, she has probably heard it all before. She has seen everything. Unlike just about every other expert telling us how we should approach sex, the Church has a *tradition*, that is, a long memory and a long experience of teaching about life as she has known it for two thousand years. And the Bible she holds in her lap goes back even further than she does with its memories and stories. Even if — *even if* — the Church had no claim to divine guidance, just this long memory and experience should make us think twice before writing off her opinions.

Before too many centuries had passed, the Church came to be called "The Old Woman." She knew and she knows so much. Though she might sound naïve and look fussy, she will never be as absurd as a book or a hairstyle just twenty years out-of-date. The Church might remind you of Ma Joad in John Steinbeck's great novel, *The Grapes of Wrath*. As keeper of her family, Ma Joad has a wisdom for any and every age. In that story, migrant workers traveled across the country to new fields and homes. Each night they made camp, a world they could live in only because of the laws that held it together:

> The families learned what rights must be observed — the right of privacy in the tent; the right to keep the past black hidden in the heart; the right to talk and to listen; the right to refuse help or to accept, to offer help or to decline it; the right of son to court and daughter to be courted; the right of the hungry to be fed; the rights of the pregnant and the sick to transcend all other rights.

> And the families learned, although no one told them, what rights are monstrous and must be destroyed: the right to intrude upon privacy, the right to be noisy while the camp slept, the right of seduction or rape, the rights of adultery and theft and murder. These rights were crushed, because the little worlds could not exist for even a night with such rights alive.[1]

Do we appreciate this sense of our lives as just a series of night camps on the way to someplace else? Just this the Church insists upon in preaching about pilgrimage. She has lived through so many encampments. She is old, yes, but hardly crazy. But how shallow we are to see sudden wisdom in the newest expert or the next contraceptive, which the drug companies will assure us is as safe as they told us the last one was. When they produce a new one, they can mention the dangers of the old one in order to sell this one. Surely we can find wiser and better people to consult!

Look, there are a lot of other Churches, Christian Churches, that also know a thing or two. Not too many of them go along with the Catholic Church in her teaching against divorce and against contraception. In fact, at least some of them see abortion as a tragic necessity.

The disunity of the Churches is a tragedy and a scandal, one that has gone on for a long, long time. The Catholic Church traces her roots back to Jesus and his apostolic teaching. In spite of many human weaknesses, the Catholic Church has faithfully proclaimed for 2,000 years the basic teaching of Jesus. Moreover, the Church does not believe that she has the right to change that teaching.

Saint Augustine said that many people of God were not people of the Church, and many people of the Church were not people of God. But all things being equal, he considered it very important to belong to the Catholic Church. There are many saints and great teachers in other Christian Churches. But it is also true that these Churches have not always remained faithful to the teaching of Christ and the apostles.

You speak of abortion as a "*tragic* necessity." Apparently, then, you see abortion as evil, though sometimes unavoidable evil. Many agree with you, of course. Maybe most of those who favor a right to abortion think as you do. But just take a closer look at your mind and heart, which are clearly telling you that abortion is *evil*. Leave out the words "unavoidable" or "tragic." These are only modifiers of the main word and the main point — evil. The Catholic Church refuses to make peace with this evil. And she insists upon what the Bible clearly teaches, that we cannot do ourselves or anybody else good by doing evil.

I doubt if many people really accept this "holier than thou" attitude of the Catholic Church. I for one do not.

We can only apologize for what may sometimes be arrogance. We did not learn that from Christ or from the Catholic Church. Insofar as we Catholics remember our pitiful merits along with our sense of responsibility, we might make our own these sentiments of a humble man who had a great mother:

> My mother, she was born a slave, she knew that and she pointed it out to me. "You are my first-born and I want to tell you the truth." She told me that white people feared black folks because they didn't understand them. She wanted her first-born to make a place in this world for himself and to help everybody else. "They are not going to have a mother like you have, and you owe them a debt. You will know something they don't know."[2]

We feel that in the Catholic Church we have an unusual mother. Probably you would agree that she is at least different. Sometimes we are, too. She makes us this way.

But even within herself the Catholic Church is divided, especially about some of these moral issues. If priests and theologians cannot get their acts together, why should anyone listen? I can find priests, nuns, and theologians to back up just about any view on sexual morality. There is no such thing as Catholic teaching in this area.

Are you really looking for a consensus of theologians on these issues? After all, they are merely individual experts. Do you know any group of experts — in medicine, finance, psychology, or education — who agree even on some of the most basic issues in their fields? In fact, the sciences — and theology among them — could not advance without disagreement and dispute, without arguments in learned journals and maybe even popular magazines.

If you truly seek an important consensus in matters of sexual moral teaching, you can look to the bishops of the Catholic Church with the pope at their head. They do not have their authority from brains or education, but from their place as successors of the apostles. Why look to the Catholic Church for anything else but the preaching of Jesus Christ as handed down through the centuries and voiced live today? There is no other reason to gather in church on Sundays than that one, when all is said and done. In his lifetime, Jesus *preached,* that is, he spoke for God as the prophets and John the Baptizer had spoken before him. After his Resurrection, he commissioned the apostles to carry on the same work and promised he would be with them until the end of time (Matthew 28:16-20). Those apostles commissioned successors. As the Second Vatican Council teaches, the preaching of these bishops makes up the revelation in this our day; it carries the authority of the living Christ.[3]

As Catholics we would do well to seek Christ's living views of moral life where he promised to leave his Spirit, his voice, his vision — with the successors of the apostles. Then we would be amazed at the unanimity of their teaching on matters that we might otherwise think are in dispute. We may respect individual experts and their arduous work. But we reserve our *faith* for the preaching of Jesus Christ, proclaimed in this our day by the bishops who succeed his apostles.

But I must follow my conscience. You seem to have little respect for its sacredness and my freedom to follow it. Who are you to judge?

Well said. Indeed you must follow your conscience, and only God can judge you there. We ought not intrude. We only want to point out a realm larger than your or anyone's conscience, one that confronts it with a decision between right and wrong. This is the realm of preaching, of prophecy, as anyone can read about it in both the Old and New Testaments. In this realm, human beings like Jeremiah and Ezekiel, John the Baptizer and Peter the Apostle, and above all Jesus of Nazareth stood up in God's name to tell the people how *God* saw things.

Let us consult Saint Luke's writings for a moment. In Luke 3:1-20, John the Baptizer announces God's judgment on the people. They cry out, "What ought we do?" And he tells them that they are to share their goods, be honest and kind in their dealings. In Acts 2:14-41 Peter preaches about God's judgment on his listeners. They, too, ask what they are to do, and he tells them: "You must reform and be baptized each one of you, in the name of Jesus Christ." Peter was preaching here on Pentecost day, the birthday of the Church. And in telling the story, Saint Luke leads up to this call for baptism and reform as the climax of that great day.

What about *our* day; who talks to *us?* Must we be content to read the Bible as a mere collection of instructive stories, to turn to experts who will offer us a variety of opinions, one apparently as good as another? Does anyone speak for God? Can anyone tell us how he sees things? Well, this is the responsibility the Catholic Church sees she has received from Jesus Christ. In the apostolic preaching throughout the centuries his very Word goes on. Again, the bishops are the keepers of his living message.

We are warmed by the words and sentiments of one of the great nineteenth-century thinkers, John Henry Cardinal Newman, so often quoted in the debates and speeches of the Second Vatican Council. In the last century, he found his way into the Catholic Church and her truth. He said that, in view of so much philosophical and religious confusion even in his time, it appealed to his sense of a loving God that he would provide an utterly reliable, even infallible, guide for seekers after religious truth.[4] This guide was and is the Catholic Church. We build correct consciences upon her teaching.

What, then, are we to do?

But the Holy Spirit is with the ordinary people of the Church, too. Most people do not accept what the pope and bishops say about birth control. Surely their experience and opinion count for something.

The great Cardinal Newman called attention to consulting the laity in matters of faith. You might remember that Pope Pius XII did this through the bishops when he was getting ready to declare the Assumption a dogma of our faith. He found out what he probably already knew: That ordinary Catholics believed Mary was assumed body and soul into heaven. Well, why not apply this procedure to contraception?

The response is not so clear as we Americans might expect. Many Catholics in other parts of the world are not clamoring at all for a change in the Church's view of contraception. At the Synod of Bishops in 1980, Archbishop John R. Quinn of San Francisco spoke of the American laity's general rejection of this teaching; he asked that the topic be reviewed and suggested that there might be a new development in it. But he found out that the bishops of other and poorer countries were having no difficulty with their people in this area. It is striking to note that both groups saw an issue of freedom here, but different kinds of freedom. We Americans tend to see the whole thing as an issue of freedom of conscience. But the bishops of some Third World countries feared that a religious approval of contraception would lead their governments to impose it on their people, an oppression they are already fighting off.

To tell the truth, if we look just to the issue of personal conscience, and to the personal and financial difficulties of married couples in this country, your question seems to have the upper hand. But you and all of us belong to a *universal* Church; it is unique in that. What looks so obviously good in Manhattan, New York, scares people and bishops in Bombay, India. And from Africa, where life and fertility are so joined and prized, the Synod bishops protested that they could hardly understand the problem of contraception in countries like ours![5]

Maybe we do not see so clearly as we thought. It could be that "the people" have other views than ours. To say, as even some learned people do, that the Holy Spirit is *clearly* saying something through ordinary people about contraception is just not true.

I do not live "over there." I live right here. And I know that many people are voting with their feet on the Church's views on these matters: They are leaving the Church. Or they just ignore the bishops when they are talking nonsense. Their experience is saying something!

Yes, it does say something. But what? That so many good people — those who practice contraception or remarry after divorce or seek what they consider necessary comfort outside of marriage — cannot all be wrong? They may well be good people. Let us grant that they are. But good and ordinary people do evil. And the Church insists that what she calls sin is evil, and that it will harm us and others. Yet the "experience" of so many people is supposed to prove that because it is *their* experience, it must be all right. For they are "good people."

How good? How good are any of us? Who is telling lies, the laws that say we commit sin? Or are we the liars — those of us who claim that because we are good people we cannot possibly be the kind of characters the laws have in mind? Saint Paul explains this more thoroughly in chapter seven of his Letter to the Romans. In the first part of this great Letter he takes great pains to help every single human being to see that he or she is involved in sin and evil. Why does he spend so much time on law and sin? So that every one of us can fall on Jesus Christ for safety and salvation. Listen to Jesus make the same point much more gently. When he sat down to eat with disreputable people and thereby made himself one of their company, the Pharisees made out that they were shocked. Jesus simply said, ''People who are healthy do not need a doctor; sick people do. I have come to call sinners, not the self-righteous'' (Mark 2:17).

Can we hear the urgency of the Scriptures as they insist that only truly sinful people have what it takes to have Jesus sit down with them and make himself one with them? Saint Augustine said it well: ''The first thing you must know is that you are a sinner.''

What does that really mean, that *I* am a sinner? When do I know that? I know it when some moral evil grabs me, like a rat sinking its teeth into my hand or my neck, and I cannot shake it off. As long as I can at least pretend that I can take care of my own problem — that I can end this affair, break that habit, let go of this resentment or hatred, escape from this fraud and restore what I have stolen — I can comfort myself that this good person is in charge of my life. But when I try to take charge and I cannot, what then? Then I know I need a savior.

But I can try another trick. I can blame the problem on the law or rule that accuses me. If only the authorities will change the law, then I will not be a sinner anymore. How simple! Yes, and how deceitful. Scripture has this comment:

If we say, ''We are free of the guilt of sin,''

we deceive ourselves; the truth is not to be found in us.

But if we acknowledge our sins,

he who is just can be trusted

to forgive our sins

and cleanse us from every wrong.
If we say, ''We have never sinned,''
we make him a liar
and his word finds no place in us (1 John 1:8-10).

I am afraid that much of the tradition handed on by the Catholic Church is Christianity in its worst view of life and sex. What an insult to marriage in the words you quote from Paul: Better to marry than to burn! Attitudes like this keep the Church in the Middle Ages.

We wish we could say that the Catholic Church has not suffered its own kind of fixation on sex. We priests have met just too many people who learned to see a sexual sin in everything. It seems that Catholic girls did indeed worry that patent leather shoes might mirror their underwear! But is the world's flaunting of sex in magazines and movies any more wholesome? And do words like Saint Paul's really mean what he said, or what in our own obsessions we hear them to mean?

Saint Paul meant that marriage offered, as the medievals put it, a remedy for concupiscence, which might sound worse still. But if we understood what the medieval theologians meant by concupiscence, we would probably agree with them. They took concupiscence to be the wound and confusion of our sinful human nature, which allows and even incites our desires and needs to run away with us, like a car with its accelerator stuck. In the blessing of marriage, man and woman could find a peace they sought and maybe knew they were looking for. An example might further the point. A priest was speaking with a widower who was finding that old sexual fears were coming back to prey on him now that he had lost his wife. But the man was not yearning for her as a sexual receptacle and release, but as a friend who had helped gather fragments of him into one peaceful self. He was missing — her.

Footnotes

1. John Steinbeck, *The Grapes of Wrath* (New York: Penguin Books, 1976), pp. 213-214.
2. Studs Terkel, *American Dreams: Lost and Found* (New York: Pantheon Books, 1980), pp. 26-27.
3. Austin Flannery, O.P., ed., *Vatican Council II: The Conciliar and Post Conciliar Documents* (Northport: Costello Publishing, 1975), pp. 753-754.
4. John Henry Cardinal Newman, *Apologia Pro Vita Sua* (New York: Longmans, Green, and Co., 1890), pp. 241-247.
5. This information comes from Jan Grootaers and Joseph A. Selling, *The 1980 Synod of Bishops "On the Role of the Family"* (Leuven: University Press, 1983), pp. 26, 57-60, 92-96.

THREE

What's So Sacred About Marriage?

Husbands, love your wives, as Christ loved the church. He gave himself up for her to make her holy, purifying her in the bath of water by the power of the word, to present to himself a glorious church, holy and immaculate, without stain or wrinkle or anything of that sort. Husbands should love their wives as they do their own bodies. He who loves his wife loves himself. Observe that no one ever hates his own flesh; no, he nourishes it and takes care of it as Christ cares for the church — for we are members of his body.

"For this reason a man shall leave his father and mother,
   and shall cling to his wife,
   and the two shall be made into one."

This is a great foreshadowing; I mean that it refers to Christ and the Church. In any case, each one should love his wife as he loves himself, the wife for her part showing respect for her husband (Ephesians 5:25-33).

I noticed you skipped what came just before that selection from the Scripture. You skipped Paul's telling wives to be submissive to their husbands. How can anyone explain this Christian abasement of women?

Just like you — to notice what was skipped! But the problem you raise is too big and visible for anyone to think no one would notice it, as no one might notice that just one page had been removed from a large book. We limited ourselves to the selection above because it contains the main point and the context in which to understand "Wives, be submissive to your husbands." From that one sentence some preachers weave a large piece of the pattern of the relationship of husband and wife. They misuse the Scripture.

Speaking from the tradition of the Church, Pope John Paul II says this to husbands:

> Authentic conjugal love presupposes and requires that a man have a profound respect for the equal dignity of his wife: "You are not her master," writes St. Ambrose, "but her husband; she was not given to you to be your slave, but your wife. . . . Reciprocate her attentiveness to you and be grateful to her for her love." With his wife a man should live "a very special form of personal friendship."[1]

We said that the quote from Ephesians provides the context for understanding Saint Paul's call for wives to be submissive to their husbands. Such husbands would be loving their wives as their own bodies and their own selves. They would be loving their wives as Christ Jesus loves his Church, and would be earning their wives' affection as Christ has earned ours. Moreover, Saint Paul also has a humbling for the men of the household when he points out that Christ gave his life up for the Church. The cry heard in time of shipwreck or fire, "Women and children first" directs menfolk to their responsibility and also their *dispensability*. When as human family or human race, man, woman, and child confront the tiger or the bear, or the fire or the enemy, one is strong enough physically and dispensable enough overall to go out and die. Like Christ for us, the husband is servant and sacrifice for his wife and children.

All of this is very spiritual, and I am afraid it is too much for me. I have been married for eighteen years, have three kids, and I can tell you that Christ's love for his Church seems a million miles away from married life and me.

It sounds as though a lot of what you do may have lost its meaning for you — working, paying bills, trying to understand your spouse, waiting up for your teenagers to come home safe at night. You may be tired, probably are. But you may also have lost sight of how your life makes sense, fits into something bigger and more important than you are. A lot of us, unfortunately, wake up one day and ask ourselves in the words of a popular song, "Is that all there is?" And from that day on we begin to get through our lives rather than live them.

Religion stands or falls by providing or failing to provide meaning for our daily lives. Its job is to show us about even the littlest and most ordinary and most painful parts of our lives, that within them and behind them lies something else. Religion says, "No, that is not all there is."

Does your wedding day sometimes seem like a joke to you, or a joke *on* you? What a day! Maybe we can sum up everything about it by calling it a day of promises. You promised — "Till death do us part." Your spouse did, too. And it must have seemed that God himself made promises, too. Did it seem he told you that you would find life and joy in your marriage and your family? Does God make us promises? Oh yes!

The Bible calls them "covenants," though for us the word "promises" sounds warmer, closer, more personal. In the very beginning, even knowing how they would turn out, God made man and woman. Was he playing a bad joke on them? No, he made them a promise of life and renewal even after they had sinned, a promise he has kept through the ages. God makes promises to us; he always keeps them. We make promises, too. But how often we break them! No matter what we do, God must keep his promises. Otherwise he would not be God.

In the scriptural passage at the head of this chapter, Saint Paul identifies the union — even the sexual union — of man and wife with the union of Jesus and his Church. We would miss the force of this if we envision cathedrals, popes, contemplative nuns, and holy Mass-goers as this Church. This Church is all kinds of people, good and bad, whom Christ has embraced in an unbreakable promise. Saint Paul says about the two becoming one flesh that it is a great "foreshadowing" ("mystery" is the word in the original Greek) that has to do with Jesus and the Church.

Do you know why, most basically, Christian sacramental marriage can never be dissolved? It is not because of the dignity of persons or the bond of a contract or the good of the children and of society; it is because of Jesus' embrace of humankind in his Church. So your marriage is a sacrament, that is, a sign or suggestion of *the real thing* — God's marriage with us poor human beings. You are part of that. You suffer for that. The grace or the strength and peace you pray for comes as a share in that divine wedding.

My wife has left me and the kids. She has taken up with someone else — just moved in with him. I want her back. My friends say I am crazy, I should just give it up. Do you think I am crazy? Do you think I can love her back?

Life should have taught all of us by now that anything is possible, that anything can happen. But the sacrament of your marriage deepens that hope for someone like you. Your marriage and your love of your wife share in the power of Jesus Christ's promise to his Church that he will always love her, pursue her when she might be unfaithful, and somehow have her home again with him, to love him and be loved by him. What you feel for your wife is not just your own sentiment and passion, but also a welling up of God's eternal embrace of us poor human beings. He will not and cannot let us go any more than you can write off your wife.

Your friends mean well. They see your pain and advise a "reasonable" course to relieve it. But do they understand your passion as a gift of God? Can they believe about a human being or even about God that "forever" can really mean what it says? God gives us people like you to help us understand how hopelessly he is in love with us. This is another reason why your marriage is a sacrament, meaning *sign,* a cloudy photograph of the heart of God.

But love does not conquer all. Still, it does believe all things, hope all things, endure all things (1 Corinthians 13:7), just as you try to do with your beloved. Try as he did, Jesus failed to win to himself his own people and even his own disciples. Remember that when Jesus was arrested, Peter denied he ever knew him. Probably you will fail, too; your wife will probably not come back. Your friends know that and want to spare you what they see as useless pain. When Jesus could not conquer the hearts and minds of his disciples and his people, he pushed on to what we call his "Passion." His love drove him to die upon the Cross. It made no more sense to those disciples and people than your passion does to your friends.

No, you are not crazy.

Am I hung up on sex in my marriage? My husband loves me; I think I can count on that. But I sometimes feel so *used* sexually. I often resist his sexual attention to me. I hate to be pretending about making love. Is there something wrong with me?

Probably very many women feel the way you do, whether for the same reasons or not. At any rate, they will sometimes mention this to a priest, worried that they are denying their husbands due affection and sexual expression of it. They talk about feeling one way and having to act another.

In your question you speak about — "pretending." You say also that you sometimes feel "used." At worst, some women have said they feel like mere receptacles for the discharge of a man's tension. Or they may resent a husband's lack of attentiveness and romance. They may carry disappointment about him, his failures, his personal limitations. For these women the sexual embrace becomes apparently a pretense, an embarrassment, and a cause of deepening anger.

Maybe you can talk to your husband. He might understand you and then be able to improve the way he relates to you. But remember that he is just a man, and *this* man, not anyone else or everyone else. Even if he is burdened by deep flaws that sometimes weigh painfully on you, you see that he is probably doing the best he can.

It might be as bad as this, however, that he will not even *try* to listen and meet your needs better than he does. Is there anything you can do, if he can or will do nothing? Yes. Some women have discovered something and others have understood it when they heard it.

As an embrace, intercourse expresses *acceptance*. Two become one — "flesh of my flesh and bone of my bone," as Adam described it. Especially is it acceptance for the woman. In her body she opens herself and brings into herself the man she embraces. But suppose she has mixed feelings about him and about life with him? Does she have to lie to herself? No. She can openly embrace *this* man, as he is, good or bad, kind or unkind, successful or not. If she can help him to change for the better, she should try. But for now her life is this way and not another, and she can truthfully open herself to it as she takes it in her arms. No lie here, but *acceptance* — the truth.

I think my wife could make our sex life more interesting. She seems to be against trying anything different. Is there something immoral about the way I think?

Probably for centuries confessors asked that kind of question have responded with one simple point: As long as intercourse is properly carried out, all the other acts and attitudes connected with it are not to be considered immoral. So a man and his wife have ample liberty for variations of sexual expression.

But as we have already noted, the focus of marriage is not the body in a narrow physical sense. In marriage two people make the gift of one to the other as *persons* — individual, unique persons. Maybe your wife has worried about the morality of some kinds of lovemaking. You can calm her conscience about that. But you still have to deal with her individual feelings in a most tender area of your life together. Sex can be exciting. God made it that way. But he also made it to express love and union. That love may require you to abstain from things that would not offend morality but would offend her feelings.

I keep thinking about another man, not my husband. My feelings all run toward him. I think my heart is telling me something. I am scared.

A priest often hears this, especially in confession. The following response seems to make sense to people.

Whether or not you have become sexually involved with this other man, there remains — and will remain till you decide to do something about it — this difference between him and your husband. You *chose* your husband, as he chose you. You sealed this choice by a promise, and built your marriage upon it. No one can build a marriage on *feelings;* they keep changing.

Many, many people who have made promises — priests, too — must wrestle with unruly feelings. Even in their fear, how calmly people have answered a priest's question whether they still choose their spouse. "Yes. Yes, I do."

On the occasion of his fortieth wedding anniversary, the husband was asked by a priest whether he wanted to renew his marriage vows with his wife. "No," he said. "I did that once, and I meant it." Most of the rest of us, however, have to keep choosing again, more deeply, more permanently. Our wandering hearts seek a warm abode. They can always go back home and shut the door a little firmer.

I am a married man. I have been faithful to my wife. Is there any harm in looking at those magazines — you know, "girlie" magazines? What about going to see one of those "girlie" shows or movies?

You are talking about pornography. We could limit this discussion to the connection of your pornography with your sexual relationship with your wife. If it would do no more than add to your excitement and hers, it probably would do you no harm. But then again, maybe you *are* doing harm. Suppose you are embracing your wife while thinking of a porno queen? Do you think your wife cannot sense something like that? Well, wives sometimes can!

But you have a worse problem. Pornography is big business — a mob-infested industry that will devour even child prostitutes to provide thrills for paying customers. Would you do that to kids? Of course not. You may have children of your own. The money you pay for magazines, burlesque shows, and movies winds up in the same bankroll that sets up the filthiest and most violent sex you can think of. In fact, if you do go back to those places, take a closer look at what is available. Better than that, get a copy of the report from the Attorney General's Commission on Pornography from the Government Printing Office.[2]

You mentioned your wife. Yes, let us talk about her. How would you like her to watch you at the nude shows? Those stomping, gyrating women are her sisters, you know. Not blood sisters, but you know what the word means. But come to think of it, they are truly sisters and daughters and mothers to some people. Your wife's feelings as she watches you there — what might they be?

A few years ago a female reporter joined a tour of the places you talk about. The tour group was composed of all women, feminists who were studying the pornography they rightly feared and hated. They made the rounds of the magazine racks and the squalid twenty-five cent movie booths. They also paid to see a stripper on a circular stage surrounded by windows or doors that one could open and look through — and grope through. The reporter watched the girl, even spoke to her. "It's a living," the girl said. The reporter could see the other windows, too. She found herself pressing herself against the back wall of her booth. What was it she shrank from seeing? The girl? No, she realized, it was not the girl. She had even spoken with her.

Later, after the tour had finished and all the women had swiftly and silently departed, she realized what she did not want to see. Now, reporters are tough people and this one said as much about herself. They are trained to observe and to remember what they see. Yet, as she walked away she realized she could not remember seeing *even one man* among all the pornography. Of course, she knew her eyes had fallen on many, very many. But she had not been able to bring herself to watch even one man leering at the likes of the girl on the stage.

So do not worry about your wife's watching you at those shows. Like that lady reporter, she would not be able to see you.

I am divorced. It was my fault. I was neglectful, unfaithful, uncaring. It is long over. Now I see ever more clearly what I have done wrong. How can I live with my unfaithfulness?

Only God is the faithful one. The Bible tells one long story of his faithfulness and his people's unfaithfulness. Your company is legion!

Remember that the sacrament that you fractured is only a sign of the faithfulness, of the everlasting promise of God. Jesus himself tells us that when this world finally passes, marriage will pass, too (Matthew 22:30). His love for us will remain the real thing. In creating you, he did not call you to destruction or to serve merely as a horrible example. Though you may have abandoned him, he cannot forget you. One way or the other, he means to see you through to salvation. He will make even your sins serve his promise of life, so long as you confess and repent of them.

You groan under the weight of your sins and the guilt of them. Give all that to the Lord Jesus, the Lamb of God who takes away the sins of all of us. Take a little time with these passages in the Bible that speak of God's taking away our guilt: Isaiah 53:11-12; Ezekiel 18:30-32; Micah 7:18-19.

Your question indicates that God's work of salvation is well under way in you. You speak humbly, maybe even wisely. You see more clearly. Do you find yourself judging others more gently, as you hope God will judge you? Well, these changes in you are small sacraments, too, signs that he has not thrown you off but draws you closer to him. Let your unfaithfulness praise his faithfulness!

I am divorced, too. I have remarried outside the Church. I feel I am doing the best I can in this situation. Why am I not allowed to receive Communion? And I do not appreciate anyone's saying of me that I am living in sin!

As a figure of speech it has its uses — living in sin — but as a judgment on you or anyone, it offends God. Only *he* can make that judgment, and only you can speak out of your own conscience about your relationship with him.

You may well be a holier person than some Catholics who rightfully go to Communion. But so are saintly Protestants. Most basically the denial of Catholic Holy Communion to you and them rests on something other than a judgment on the state of your soul.

The Eucharist, too, is a sacrament, a sign of Christ's presence. And our receiving it is a *sign* of our union with him and with his body, the Church. Pope John Paul II, in reaffirming the Church's practice, says that the divorced and remarried may not be admitted to the Eucharist because "their state and condition of life objectively contradict the union of love between Christ and the Church which is signified and effected by the Eucharist." No one rejoices in this state of affairs, which makes it so clear that something has gone wrong and ought to be set right. But we cannot set things right by just pretending with Holy Communion that we enjoy unity and mutual recognition when we do not. Holy Communion says "Unity!" We cannot tell lies.

Note, however, that exclusion from Communion, painful as it is, does not mean you are excommunicated, or expelled, from the Catholic Church. You are a Catholic; you are urged and obliged to attend Sunday Mass. Many parishes have people like you devotedly involved with their worship, work, and social life. I hope you will join them.

I like the idea that sex makes promises. But why does the Catholic Church keep carrying on about "bad thoughts" and other such nonsense? I really had the daylights scared out of me about all that when I was a kid. But maybe the Church has toned these things down. I hope so.

Many have suffered as you have from an oppresive conscience or from overstrict parents or teachers. The next question has more to say about thoughts and feelings — which of themselves are *not* sins. But for now let us turn to the Catholic Church's warning against indulging in sexual fantasies and memories. As usual, you can trace her teaching back to the Scriptures and here especially to the words of Jesus Christ. Once he reminded his hearers of the commandment, ''You shall not commit adultery,'' which is often hard enough by itself. But he went on: ''What I say to you is: anyone who looks lustfully at a woman has already committed adultery with her in his thoughts'' (Matthew 5:28).

Why did he press things so far, not just about this, but also about anger, which he linked with murder (Matthew 5:22)? Because he knew that evil has its real home in the human heart, and he wanted to scour all evil from our hearts and make them new. He dealt with the question of what makes a human being evil or impure in the following passage:

''What emerges from within a man, that and nothing else is what makes him impure. Wicked designs come from the deep recesses of the heart: acts of fornication, theft, murder, adulterous conduct, greed, maliciousness, deceit, sensuality, envy, blasphemy, arrogance, an obtuse spirit. All these evils come from within and render a man impure'' (Mark 7:20-23).

Can any of us deny the fact that our evil deeds were first hatched and warmed in a secret corner of our mind and heart? How careful we must be of our first thoughts and impulses. If we allow them to breed and grow, or pretend we do not notice them, how shocked we may be one day at the evil we say or do. Jesus knew what he was talking about. We do, too.

I get the idea from what you say that the Church does not see sins everywhere in sex.

Of course not! From the time of Saint Augustine, and even before, this formula has served as a foundation of Catholic moral teaching: Whatever is of nature cannot be sinful in itself. Sexual feelings and thoughts can be powerful, even scary. But they rise from a human nature given by God. What he has made cannot be evil.

Unfortunately, many people get the idea that any thought or imagining or physical stirring displeases the God who installed these powers in their minds and bodies! They confuse the unruliness and disorder of their experience with sin in the strict sense. What they experience the Church has long called "concupiscence," which she says has its root in original sin and inclines us toward personal sin. Original sin, of course, is the common taint of the human race and the sense we all have that something is out of order. We inherit it like a family weakness. Personal sin, on the other hand, is a choice we make, and we must take responsibility for it. We sin personally when we *choose* what is forbidden to us. A man may feel attracted to someone else's wife, find her on his mind quite a lot. He does not sin in that. But if he *chooses* to dwell on or act on his thoughts and feelings, if he tries to seduce her, then he sins. If he *deliberately* fantasizes about going to bed with her, then he sins. Sin is basically in the will.

Whatever is of nature cannot be evil. Reflection on Jesus makes this point even more powerfully. Clearly he liked women and they liked him. Clearly he loved children and they flocked to him. Clearly, then, he was a sexual being. If not, he was defective. What do we feel about human beings who apparently have no sexual feelings and responses? We feel that they are tragically deprived. If they are our children and we notice lack of sexual development, we take them to a doctor and hope and pray that he can do something for them.

If Jesus was more an angel than a man, we are not saved. If God did not become like us, really like us, then he did not share our life and did not save us. But the Scripture insists that he became like us in *everything* except sin (see Hebrews 4:15). In his human body we can know that everything God has placed in our bodies is good, very good. The next chapter will have more to say about the holiness of the body.

Footnotes

1. John Paul II, *The Role of the Christian Family in the Modern World* (Boston: St. Paul Editions, n.d.), p. 42.
2. *The New York Times,* July 10, 1986, reported on these and other findings of the report of the Attorney General's Commission on Pornography. The Commission's report is available from the Government Printing Office for $35.

FOUR

Who Says My Body Is a Temple of the Holy Spirit?

"Everything is lawful for me" — but that does not mean that everything is good for me. "Everything is lawful for me" — but I will not let myself be enslaved by anything. "Food is for the stomach and the stomach for food, and God will do away with them both in the end" — but the body is not for immorality; it is for the Lord, and the Lord is for the body. God, who raised up the Lord, will raise us also by his power.

Do you not see that your bodies are members of Christ? Would you have me take Christ's members and make them the members of a prostitute? God forbid! Can you not see that the man who is joined to a prostitute becomes one body with her? Scripture says, "The two shall become one flesh." But whoever is joined to the Lord becomes one spirit with him. Shun lewd conduct. Every other sin a man commits is outside his body, but the fornicator sins against his own body. You must know that your body is a temple of the Holy Spirit, who is within — the Spirit you have received from God. You are not your own. You have been purchased, and at a price. So glorify God in your body (1 Corinthians 6:12-20).

That passage sounds so strange. Does it say anything to me today?

It begins by saying, "Everything is lawful for me." That speaks of the Christian promise of freedom. In another place, Saint Paul says, "Remember that you have been called to live in freedom — but not a freedom that gives free rein to the flesh" (Galatians 5:13). He was worried that people would trade in one kind of slavery for another: preoccupation with laws and rules for the drives of the flesh. We should be so worried! Like wayward children, so many of us have found out that we *can* commit adultery, sleep around before marriage, masturbate — and we do not die! We overlook, however, that our newfound power becomes like atomic energy, which makes us tremble to think of bombs and missiles and Chernobyl and Three Mile Island.

Paul apparently quotes a proverb of his time: "Food for the stomach and stomach for the food." People applied it to sex. But they forgot — as we forget — that sexuality is not a thing, as the stomach is. Sex is intimate and personal in a way that the stomach and eating can never be. To compare sex with eating, a function we cannot forego, makes having sex look like "no big deal." We can pretend it is "no big deal" by making it faceless. In prostitution and pornography, faces do not matter because the person does not matter. So we call this kind of sex "obscene" because it is out-of-place and has nothing to do with personal relationships.

But a Christian cannot approach sex that way and be a follower of Christ; for a Christian's body is destined for resurrection. Our Christian faith does not believe in survival after death in the filmy way other people speak of it. We believe in the resurrection of the body because the Bible cannot conceive of a human person disembodied. As a Christian, my body is *me*. Moreover, the Christian in his or her body is a member of Jesus Christ, like a limb of a larger body! The Christian in his or her body is a temple of God, a house of worship.

And another's body is no mere thing, either, even if that other is a prostitute. In unchastity the Christian is joined to the prostitute just as in the chastity of married or single life the Christian is joined to Christ. Sex is always an event, never just ''no big deal.''

Finally, Paul leaps over the argument of whose body mine is, anyway, by ascending to the place of redemption, where Christ died to save us, and to the place of daily life, where in our labor, grief, play, and joy we praise God in and through our bodies, our very selves. Basically, he establishes that no one's body is owned by anyone but God. This amounts to a declaration of the freedom that feminists often rightly seek when they declare it demeaning that men should treat women in their bodies as their property and possession.

I am eighteen. I love a boy who loves me too. I have had sex with him. Maybe I should feel bad about this, but I do not. Not that it has been ''no big deal.'' It means very much to me and to him.

What a happy thing to know, to really know as you do now, that sex is not dirty. Unfortunately, some people seem never to appreciate that. Maybe we can reflect further on your experience in order to deepen your moral awareness.

Was it not true that in your embrace you and your boyfriend felt you were saying to each other, ''You and only you for me, and I for you — forever''? (Just about all the young people we priests talk to seem to feel that way.) Well, your moral problem is staring you in the face: What you felt yourself saying you were not saying at all. It was not forever, not just each one for just the other. You were telling each other lies! And until the time might come for the two of you to stand up and tell each other the truth, to make the real promises of marriage, you will continue to tell lies. No one can keep telling lies without being corrupted.

You know now that sex *says* things, and says them powerfully. If it were true that sex said nothing, or if people did not feel what you feel, then sex would be utterly insignificant, a stop at something like a hamburger joint — "no big deal." People can learn to "sleep around"; that is, they can *unlearn* the language of sexual intimacy. They can learn not to feel what has so thrilled you in your recent sexual experience.

Treasure what you have. Thank God for what you have learned, even at the price of sin. The Lord God lovingly pays that price for you, whom he created to make love and make promises at the same time.

Of all the Catholic Church's positions on sexual morality, the one I least understand is the one on contraception — birth control.

You might be surprised to know the limits of the Church's prohibition of artificial birth control, or contraception. She does not deny a population problem in the world. She does not deny the freedom of parents to limit their families. In the famous letter, *Humanae Vitae*, in which Pope Paul VI condemned contraception, he took note of "responsible parenthood."

> In relation to physical, economic, psychological and social conditions, responsible parenthood is exercised, either by the deliberate and generous decision to raise a numerous family, or by the decision, made for grave motives and with due respect for the moral law, to avoid for the time being, or even for an indeterminate period, a new birth.[1]

The Catholic Church is not telling us to have lots of babies since there are no family, financial, health, or population problems. She merely says to us: In struggling with real personal, family, and worldwide problems, do not make the mistake of seeing contraception as a solution.

I just cannot understand how the Catholic Church can say she understands the world's population problem and yet prohibits contraception.

In 1965, President Lyndon Johnson declared that five dollars spent on population control was as good as five hundred spent on developing the economic well-being of a poorer country. This obvious bargain in buying a way out of the world's population and food problems seems to make so much sense to us. But much of the rest of our world noted what Johnson said and resented him for it. In their view, the wastefulness of richer countries like the United States consumes more resources than do the populations of countries in South America and Asia. And they believe that a population policy based on contraception means that wealthier nations intend to keep eating and hoarding as much as ever, while cutting back the number of people who might challenge their luxury.

For twenty years or more, the Catholic Church has insisted that the world can effectively control population only in an effort to bring all peoples up to a decent standard of living. In August of 1984, the United Nations held its International Conference on Population in Mexico City. At a preparatory meeting, Monsignor James McHugh made this point for the Holy See:

> The Holy See takes note of the emphasis on socio-economic transformation as a primary basis for any population policy. The Holy See agrees that a population policy should be part of a larger commitment to social justice and to socio-economic development that enables all persons to lead a fully human life. . . . Socio-economic development allows families and couples to make free and responsible decisions about family life and parenthood.[2]

In fact, people in desperate poverty have little or no control over the size of their families, or anything else either. In one desperately poor country now trying to reforest its hillsides and reclaim its soil, goats eat up trees and seedlings right away. Well, why not kill off the goats until the job is done? Because the goats mean today's milk and tonight's supper for starving stomachs and hollow eyes that have no energy to see past sunset. These people are just trying to stay alive, one day at a time. They cannot even comprehend the longer view that we can take in ordering our lives because we have money in the bank and food in the freezer. They cannot plan their menus or their families.

The Catholic Church's position on this matter has made a deep impression. At the United Nations population conference of 1974, John D. Rockefeller, former chairman of the United States population commission and a supporter for forty years of a contraceptive approach to population problems, had this to say:

> I have now changed my mind. . . . The evidence has been mounting, particularly in the past decade, to indicate that family planning alone is not adequate. . . .
>
> This approach recognizes that rapid population growth is only one among many problems facing most countries, that it is a multiplier and intensifier of other problems rather than the cause of them. And it recognizes that *motivation for family planning is best stimulated by hope that living conditions and opportunities in general will improve*[3] (italics added).

In short, then, the Church says that an approach like President Johnson's is immoral and unjust, and that it will not work. If people are to plan their families freely and responsibly, they must have a decent standard of living. And wealthier peoples have a basic responsibility to help them to achieve this standard with a sharing of the technology, goods, and wealth that is God's gift to all the peoples of the earth.

What is so wrong with contraception as a personal choice? Just about nobody else seems to have the Catholic Church's view of it. What is so wrong with it?

All of us have trouble sometimes in seeing the wrong in contraception. We priests, too, sympathize with the plight of a couple who struggles with this issue. We know they probably cannot understand why the Catholic Church insists upon the evil of contraception. Maybe we can catch a glimpse of the evil she sees, which so easily deceives our eyes.

As we have said before, the Church has been around for a long, long time. She has had to combat contraception before. In the course of the ages, especially when defending the endangered dignity of woman and the sacredness of the lives of fetuses and infants, she has laid out a three-point bulwark: no divorce, no abortion, no contraception. Like a general defending a city, she has feared that the loss of any one of the three defenses would cause the collapse of the other two. How naïve of us to think that the current attacks on all three positions are not part of the same war. And though we might disagree with the Church and plan to gain some respite from the siege if we yield on contraception (not essential, we think), we have to admit that she has fought this battle several times before and might know something that we do not.

And the worst lie we Catholics tell ourselves about contraception is that we know the difference between that and what the pro-abortionists promote and do. How did abortion gain its approval in American law? By following on the legal principles set up by our society's acceptance of contraception, especially the principle of the right to privacy. And do we not know of the successful efforts of pro-abortionists to have people accept abortion as another form of contraception? And do we not know how contraceptive pills work? They are designed to do several things, and one of them is to prevent implantation of the developing embryo in the mother's womb. A prominent abortion activist has noticed this puzzling — and maybe willful — ignorance:

I know many people who are strongly anti-abortion who use the Pill, and have no problem with the third function of

51

the Pill, which is to alter the endometrium (and cause an early abortion). . . . They are absolutely astounded and amazed that you would begin to call the Pill both a true contraceptive and a true abortifacient.[4]

The Catholic Church is not surprised to see the beginning of the collapse of her defense against abortion, since so many have yielded the defense against contraception. The Church pleads with us to see that she prohibits contraception because it is evil. In the end, evil can only do us harm.

When people talk about "the contraceptive mentality," what do they mean?

Probably no one has ever firmly defined it. As a frame of mind, it would be hard to pin down, anyway. A person of this mind looks to gain as complete control over life as possible, so as to have it serve his or her purposes and pleasures. Contraceptives fit into this project by enabling such a one to use sex — within or without marriage — while maintaining complete control over a conception that might interfere with other plans. The other plans may be to marry someone other than this sexual partner, or to buy a foreign sports car, or to invest in the finest of educations for children already born.

But do not understand this to say that everyone who uses contraceptives does so out of self-centeredness. Sometimes good and generous people can see no alternative to contraceptives, at least for a time. (The next question touches on this.) And some who do not use them at all can still be steeped in a contraceptive mentality.

What is wrong with such a mentality? For one thing, it takes an unreasonable approach to life, which cannot be fully controlled. For life is full of surprises. To say the same thing on a religious level, it sniffs at our Lord's words on the lilies of the field and the birds of the air and God's care of them (see Matthew 6:26-34). People who believe they have their lives fully under control do not need God to take care of them. Moreover, they often have little sense of owing anything to life or anything else. Our Lord spoke of such people in the parable of the silver pieces, or the "talents" (see Matthew 25:14-30). Remember the dull fellow who buried his thousand silver pieces, or talents, because he was afraid of losing them? His lord condemned him for failing at least to let the money out to bankers so as to gain some interest for the lord. But he would not let go of anything in any way; he would keep things utterly under control! This parable speaks about a selfish waste of life, which amounts to the contraceptive mentality.

At first glance, such a waste of life may look very rigorous and vital. Behold the "yuppies," stylishly jogging, dieting, and lifting weights, as they strain to hold onto youth and beauty! Watch them suck life like an orange for its last drop of juice, and notice how little of life or treasure they give back or give away. See them jump into their BMWs to race to their trendy pubs, and hear the bartenders grumble about the low tips these people leave!

This mentality and the use of contraceptives can also lead to violence. Sometimes it is directed against oneself in sterilization. Is it not tragic to realize that thousands and thousands of young people in our country cannot have children? True, they will respond, "I chose this." But is the fact any less tragic, that this person is no longer physically capable of having children? That they seem not to feel it underscores the loss of vitality, the deadness of it all. A journalist, Robert J. Samuelson, sensed this deadness, especially after parenting his first child at the age of thirty-nine. He wrote, "The truth is . . . that I'm part of the baby bust. . . . Like others of our generation, my wife and I have yet to reproduce ourselves. Collectively, this is an ominous failure."[5]

The contraceptive mentality also drifts by deadly logic toward the violence of abortion. For one who wants to maintain full control, contraception is not enough. Listen to this statement:

Women have always used abortion as a means of fertility control. Unless we ourselves can decide whether and when to have children, it is difficult for us to control our lives or participate fully in society. . . .

Since no birth control method is 100 percent effective, abortion is a necessary backup when birth control fails.[6]

We have to provide contraceptives to our teenagers. They are having sex, no matter what we might wish or want to believe, and they will have sex. I think it is irrational, then, not to provide them with the means to responsible use of sex, so as to avoid pregnancy and venereal disease. What a tragedy teenage pregnancy has become in our country!

Planned Parenthood has been taking your approach for years. Yet many people have been noticing that programs to provide contraceptive information and techniques have not been doing much good. Some even think this approach has made the problem worse!

Frank Furstenberg, a University of Pennsylvania sociologist and expert in teenage pregnancy, does not think that adolescents will hold to virginity rather than use contraceptives in the years before they marry. But he would still like to see the growing number of "say no" programs given a try because sex lectures and pills have had hardly any impact on the numbers of teenage pregnancies.[7]

You know, you sound like a crusader. Planned Parenthood does, too, as its members toil on behalf of their vision of teenage America and scorn those who oppose them as hopelessly benighted. But you see, our view is that you are giving our teenagers over to *evil* when you give them contraceptives and at least imply that unchastity does not matter much. Note two things about evil: It does not work and if you look at it long enough you see it does not make sense. Your approach does not work; it apparently fails to do what you want it to do — prevent teenage pregnancy and venereal disease. And it makes no sense.

Is sex for teenagers — or for anyone, for that matter — merely a physical drive connected only with pleasure, pregnancy, and the possibility of disease? What does playing at sex do *emotionally* to teenagers? What does abortion do to them emotionally? And what do contraceptives do for the very poor who generation after generation lie stuck in their destitution? Even if you succeeded in scrubbing their sex lives free of pregnancy and disease, would you really be helping them to get ahead? The eminent social-psychologist, Robert Coles, noted this about a recent survey:

> Whereas 78% of the respondents who plan to finish only "some high school" are "nonvirgins," 77% of those respondents who already know they want to go to graduate school and 76% who want to complete "all of college" are "virgins" — an almost exact reversal. Moreover, those who at the time of the survey were not doing well in school were evidently more active sexually than those who were doing well in school. . . .
>
> One wonders whether this questionnaire doesn't offer additional evidence that Freud's theory of sublimation . . . isn't correct: When energy "flows" into sexuality, it is not available for the planning and studying that make those dreams become a reality.[8]

Providing contraceptive pills to teenagers does not make sense from any angle. The teenagers often fail to take them anyway. And if they do, the pills put up no barriers to venereal disease and, in fact, probably make girls' bodies even more defenseless before the gonococcus of venereal disease.[9] You care about them, surely. Then how can you treat them that way? Our children are human beings and children of God; they have the dignity to take responsibility for their lives, their future, and their success. Chastity guards that dignity while unchastity degrades it.

I know the Church's law on contraception. Sometimes I say I reject it. But I really do not; I feel guilty. But as God is my judge, I think I am doing the best I can! I cannot do any better and hold my marriage and family together. I think sometimes that the Church comes between God and me!

You may find it hard to see, but God is clearly about the work of making you holy, even while it seems to you that you are sliding farther away from him. You really appreciate how weak you are, right? And you cling to God's love for you, do you not, believing that somehow he understands? Well, he does understand. And he is also humbling you, teaching you how weak you are and how much you need him for his strength, comfort, and forgiveness. Humility is such a lovely word, but what always leads us to it does not sound so nice — humiliation. The saints say that holiness is built first of all on humility, and that usually we find humility only in the acceptance of humiliation.

Moreover, Jesus insisted in Mark 2:17 that he came for sinful people, not the virtuous, who presumably could take care of themselves. How lightly we say it, "Of course, I am a sinner." But out of an experience like yours, we know the bitter truth about sin and about ourselves. We know we wait for Jesus, whose name means *savior*. Have you never read about and loved the tax collector who, unlike the Pharisee, could only stand at the very back of the place of prayer and plead for mercy? He could not keep the rules, and not being able to keep them thought he did not belong there. But there he found God; whereas the Pharisee, who could keep the rules, did not (Luke 18:9-14).

You see the point, surely. In your very question you were casting about for something in religion that goes deeper than laws and rules. You seek the mercy of God, which alone saves us all, which does not take its measure from how virtuous we are. Well, the price of that mercy for you and all the rest of us is the acceptance of laws and commandments that accuse us of breaking them, whether we try to keep them or not. In your case, for instance, the law against contraception causes you to appeal to God's personal understanding of you and love for you. You are seeking his mercy because you admit you are in trouble.

The Church, too, understands. Pope Paul VI spoke these compassionate words to married people:

> The awareness that one has not achieved his full interior liberty and is still at the mercy of his tendencies, and *finds himself unable to obey the moral law in an area so basic,* causes deep distress. But this is the moment in which the Christian, rather than giving way to sterile and destructive panic, humbly opens up his soul before God as a sinner before the saving love of Christ[10] (italics added).

And John Paul II has spoken of a "law of gradualness," of growth to the holiness and virtue that God calls us to. Because Christ also preached the commandments, the Holy Father rejects on the other hand a "gradualness of the law." This would amount to an ideal that would bind as law or rule only when we had developed to a certain point in moral achievement and willingness. But this would make for different levels of citizenship and discipleship in the Church and in the following of Christ. This the Church cannot allow because Christ preached the commandments and the Sermon on the Mount to *all* the people, whether they were ready to hear his words or not.

Be sure, then, that in your confusion and anguish you are meeting Christ as really and deeply as did the sinful heroes and heroines of the Gospels.

Why does the Catholic Church insist on condemning masturbation? Who gets hurt by it?

The Church insists that sex is a gift of communication between people who love each other. Masturbation is like talking to oneself. In fact, proponents of masturbation and its techniques speak of it as making love — to oneself! But sex, like flowers, is meant to speak to others. Recently, and very briefly, the floral industry put out a TV commercial urging us to send flowers to ourselves — ''for the pleasure of it.'' How silly! As everyone knows — since the florists spent a lot of advertising money to teach us — we are supposed to ''Say it with flowers.'' They surely did not mean us to say it to ourselves.

Some recent argumentation in favor of masturbation stands on a rejection of superstitious arguments against it: that it causes warts and scrambles the brain. Well, it hardly advances the level of moral discourse to say that masturbation is now a good thing because it does *not* damage skin or soften the brain, and besides that, it feels good. We might have expected that teenagers would have long ago accepted this trivial argument. But life and sex go deeper than that:

> To a surprising degree, teenagers still regard masturbation as in some way shameful. Fewer than a third (31%) said they felt no guilt when they masturbated, and a fifth (20%) felt either ''a large amount'' or ''a great deal.'' More to the point, it seems to be something that kids just don't talk about.[11]

Maybe teenagers still hear something in their hearts. So the Church teaches that deliberate, willful masturbation is a serious sin. We should note the operative words: ''deliberate, willful.'' At times in people's lives, the experience of masturbation will not be truly deliberate and willful, especially in their adolescence.

Masturbation has been a problem for me ever since I was a young girl. I try so hard, and sometimes things go well. But the problem remains. It gets me down; I feel so guilty.

Masturbation sometimes has little or nothing to do with morality, which always involves will and choice. Maybe you can gain some understanding in what follows. It seems clear that women — the same women, too — can have two different moral experiences of masturbation. The first involves willful arousal and maybe accompaniment of it with fantasy or erotic reading; it is done for pleasure. This is seriously sinful. The second is not so much the experience of choosing pleasure as of being overcome, of almost automatically releasing a tension that rose on its own. One may be asleep, or half asleep, or trying to get to sleep. Since the experience lacks clear and deliberate choice, it cannot be seriously sinful. It may be venially sinful, if some choice is involved, or not sinful at all. Just the physical experience — sensation, manipulation, release, and relaxation — does not make a sin. Sin is not in the body, made by God with all its powers, feelings, and motions. Sin is only in the will, which often does not have full control over a bodily function or cannot control it when it is already driving powerfully toward release. We do not blame ourselves for failing to suppress a sneeze, though we all know how to do that. In fact, we probably could not tell for sure whether or not our sneezes are partly deliberate or not!

But sex is another matter. Women do feel guilty, even personally soiled, in the experience even of indeliberate masturbation. While the moral law is the same for men and women, men usually do not suffer in the same way. A man's body is not the source of life in the profound way that a woman's is. The closer we get to the source of life, the more mixed up our feelings can get between what we consider sacred and what we consider dirty. Take childbirth, for instance. Once a group of teenagers were watching a film of a woman giving birth to a child in a hospital with her husband at her side. The medical personnel were cheering her effort to force the child from her vagina: ''Go! Go!'' Her husband wept and kissed and embraced her after she had succeeded and the nurses had wiped down the bloody and slimy infant and given it to her to hold. Some of the teenagers joined the film's mood of celebration. But others were clearly frightened and disgusted! Pregnancy and childbirth, menstruation, or sexual intercourse may feel very messy to a woman. That is not the same as dirty. Life is messy.

In your dejection over masturbation, watch out for this. All human beings have a tendency to punish themselves, to prove how bad they are by repeating a sin or dropping to a worse one. Judas did this in hanging himself. He despaired. Since a woman, unlike a man, can quickly repeat climaxes, she can mire herself in her despondency and prove to herself how bad she is, by continuing to masturbate. Now she *deliberately* acts, not to gain pleasure or relaxation, but to punish herself as God never would.

You have nothing to fear. If your problem does not amount to serious sin, accept what you cannot fully control and know that all natural functions are gifts of God. If you commit a sin, what is that puny thing in the sight of God's love for you? Why do we take our sins so seriously? Why do you? God loves you, even when you feel ugly. Someone has said that there is no such thing as an ugly woman. God knows.

Do you think that the Catholic Church unfairly singles out homosexuals for condemnation?

"I cannot help the way I am" — no one can argue with that statement, whether the speaker is homosexual or heterosexual. No one is condemned by the Church for sexual tendency or orientation. No one is condemned just for experiencing feelings and desires. The Catholic Church, like the Scriptures, bases its morality on decisions and acts. She teaches that sexual expression is moral only within marriage, with an openness to conception. That one simple rule — and only that — applies to everyone, married or unmarried, celibate by choice or by circumstance, homosexual or heterosexual.

Unfortunately, human beings — and churchmen among them — do not survey homosexuality with the same even abstraction. We get emotional, upset, even repulsed. Much of this turmoil is instinctive, more basic than what is religiously learned or taught. Near the end of his life, Sigmund Freud spoke of this, and what he said perhaps provides insight into why the Church insists on keeping sex linked with procreation.

It is a characteristic common to all the perversions that in them reproduction as an aim is put aside. This is actually the criterion by which we judge whether a sexual activity is perverse — if it departs from reproduction in its aims and pursues the attainment of gratification independently. You will understand therefore that the gulf and turning-point in the development of the sexual life lies at the point of its subordination to the purposes of reproduction. Everything that occurs before this conversion takes place, and everything which refuses to conform to it and serves the pursuit of gratification alone, is called by the unhonoured title of "perversion" and as such is despised.[12]

Yet all sexual experience, good or bad, frightening or gentle, ordered or disordered, is *human*. Some priests understand that better than others, and insofar as they do, they express the understanding, compassion, and acceptance of Jesus Christ, the Son of God. For God has made all human beings for love, and all obey him at least in this, that they seek this love one way or another. And maybe most priests know that no love is so perverse as to be all bad, that God can use it to lead people on to a purer, warmer, truer place.

Are you saying, then, that it is all right for me to continue to live with a homosexual lover? I have to insist he has been a great help to me. Before I met him I had a desperate round of lovers and pickups. I am much better now. Please do not quote law to me. I cannot leave him.

No priest, no mere creature for that matter, can give you an exemption from the moral law that binds us all. But can God himself exempt you if you appeal directly to him? We will come back to this. But first of all, you can refer back to a question dealt with a few pages back, a question that ends up with wondering whether the Church sometimes gets between us and God. The response to that question has to do with God's patience and with the law of gradualness that Pope John Paul II has spoken of. We are saying this to you, then, that if God can wait for you, the Catholic Church can, too. But she cannot grant you an exemption.

Can God grant it? Understandably, you rule out quoting the law to you, for the law does not bend, does not hear, does not feel. At some time in our lives none of us can bear the law, while at the same time we feel like appealing to God, its author. Maybe he will understand. He can hear, can bend. Well, why not take the matter to God directly instead of arguing with the law? No sense arguing with it. But you can and you ought to argue with God, realizing that your anger can be your best prayer.

Saint Alphonsus Liguori, Doctor of the Church, teaches that we have only two things to pray for: To see God's will and then to be willing and able to do it. Would you be willing to pray that way, to lay yourself open to him and his way? Could you say: "Lord, I am afraid to see, but I want to anyway. And then I am afraid I will turn my back on what you show me. Can you help me then to look at it and try to follow it?" This is not an easy prayer to say, is it? But many people who could never face the mere law without despair have found the grace to say it. For the keystone of our moral lives is our trusting God, our hoping that he knows and loves us personally and wants us to know and love him.

Did you ever read the novel, *Brideshead Revisited*, or see its television adaptation? In a climactic scene, the lovers Julia and Charles know they must part. They both understand why, though Julia does the speaking:

> How can I tell what I shall do? You know the whole of me. You know I'm not one for a life of mourning. I've always been bad. Probably I shall be bad again, punished again. But the worse I am, the more I need God. I can't shut myself out from His mercy. That is what it would mean: starting a life with you, without Him. One can only hope to see one step

ahead. But I saw to-day there was one thing unforgivable —
like things in the schoolroom, so bad they are unpunishable,
that only Mummy could deal with — the bad thing I was on
the point of doing, that I'm not quite bad enough to do; to set
up a rival good to God's.[13]

Julia saw, and Charles did also, that another Lover had a claim
on each of them. They were caught between loves, not between
love on one side and law on the other. Not that this allowed them to
escape the cost and pain of their tragedy. How easy it would have
been for them to scorn the law and run to each other's arms. How
well they knew now the weight of Saint Augustine's words: ''I had
rather keep ten thousand commandments than fall in love but
once.''

So if you would dare to take your case to God, face-to-face in
prayer, this is what you risk — falling in love with him as he is in
love with you. Like Julia, you well know that such a love can have
no rival.

**I mean no offense, but tell the truth. Is it really possible to be
chaste? I have tried so hard.**

The Catholic Church teaches that no one can stay right with
God, or live finally in his grace, without *special* help from him.
She also teaches that with this special help such faithfulness is
possible. Maybe in the matter of chastity more than in any other
moral challenge do people conclude, ''I just cannot do this.''

Why is this so? For one reason, because sex drives us so
powerfully. Without this enormous God-given energy, the human
race could never have survived! All through the centuries sex has
smashed through laws and customs, caused murders, riots, and
wars, sealed marriages but also broken them up, provided wonder-
ful stories of romance, tragedy, and even martyrdom. No one has
ever found it dull. And no one can doubt that this instinct for the
continuation of the human race has done its job! What you feel

throbbing in your mind, heart, and body is a power as big as the whole human race. No wonder it confuses you — confuses all of us.

Yet, unlike food and drink, sex can be absent from the life of a physically and emotionally vibrant human being. An author concerned with the place of discipline and restraint in a truly enjoyable sex life says this:

> Celibacy is a state of life known only to humans. The fact that one *can* be celibate if one chooses is an indication of the growth of freedom. Natural life has evolved from the state of determined sexuality experienced by the lower animals to a state of potential sexuality wherein human beings are free to choose to be sexual or not.[14]

But you did not ask whether you would die without sex. You asked how it is possible to live a chaste life as a married or an unmarried person. There must live on this earth some people who can do it just by making up their minds. Surely there are not many of them. Chastity is a grace of God more than it is a matter of willpower.

Yet will and grace unite like fuel and spark in the flame of chastity. Maybe you can see yourself in these words of Saint Augustine, who struggled so long for this chastity. And maybe he can help you to see that what you think is your weak will is from another viewpoint quite a determined will that refuses to let go of evil. A new Augustine was warring with this hardened will when he wrote:

> I was bound not with the iron of another's chains, but by my own iron will. The enemy held my will; and of it he made a chain and bound me. Because my will was perverse it changed to lust, and lust yielded to become habit, and habit not resisted became necessity. These were like links hanging one on another — which is why I have called it a chain — and their hard bondage held me bound hand and foot. The new will which I now began to have, by which I willed to worship

You freely and to enjoy You, O God, the only certain Joy, was not yet strong enough to overcome that earlier will rooted deep through the years. My two wills, one old, one new, one carnal, one spiritual, were in conflict and in their conflict wasted my soul.[15]

How, then, will any one of us become chaste? By making up our minds — so long as we remember that the power to do this comes from God as a special grace. Do you want to be chaste — *really* want to? Then you will be. Saint Alphonsus Liguori reflected on Saint Augustine's long struggle and his realization that if he willed it, he could immediately be a friend of God. Alphonsus wrote the reason for this: "Because whoever wishes, with a true and resolute desire for the friendship of God, instantly obtains it." But he insisted that this must amount to "a true and resolute desire."

How do you know you have such a desire, such a will to really get down to loving God above all else? First of all, by telling him as sincerely as you can that you want to love him that way. Tell him you give yourself to him totally. Tell him you want him to remove anything from your life that gets between him and you. Second, make up your mind to avoid the "occasions of sin" — those relationships, places, magazines, films, fantasies, etc., that get you into trouble. Third, remember to say a prayer when you are tempted. And fourth, say three Hail Mary's every day to beg our Lady for the gift of chastity. Sooner or later it will be yours.

Footnotes

1. Pope Paul VI, *Humanae Vitae* (United States Catholic Conference, 1968), #10.
2. *Origins,* 13 (1984), pp. 587-588.
3. This statement of John D. Rockefeller is cited by Allan Chase, *The Legacy of Malthus* (New York: Alfred A. Knopf, 1977), pp. 430-431.
4. Correspondence, *Commonweal* 113 (1986), p. 194.

5. *Newsweek,* January 13, 1986.
6. The Boston Women's Health Book Collective, *The New Our Bodies, Ourselves* (New York: Simon and Schuster, Inc., 1984), p. 291.
7. Dr. Furstenberg is cited in *The Sunday Register* (Shrewsbury, New Jersey), July 6, 1986.
8. Robert Coles and Geoffrey Stokes, *Sex and the American Teenager* (New York: Harper and Row, 1985), p. 203. This work comments on a survey done by *Rolling Stone* magazine.
9. The Boston Women's Health Book Collective, *Our Bodies, Ourselves: A Book by and for Women,* 2nd ed. rev. (New York: Simon and Schuster, Inc., 1976), p. 191.
10. Pope Paul VI as quoted in *The Tablet* (Brooklyn), November 29, 1980.
11. Coles and Stokes, p. 65.
12. Sigmund Freud, *A General Introduction to Psycho-Analysis,* trans. Joan Riviere (New York: Simon and Schuster, Inc., 1963), p. 277.
13. Evelyn Waugh, *Brideshead Revisited* (Boston: Little, Brown and Company, 1945), p. 340.
14. Gabrielle Brown, *The New Celibacy* (New York: McGraw-Hill, 1980), p. 21.
15. *The Confessions of St. Augustine,* trans. F. J. Sheed (New York: Sheed and Ward, 1943), p. 164.

FIVE

Is Heaven for Virgins Only?

I tell you, brothers, the time is short. From now on those with wives should live as though they had none; those who weep should live as though they were not weeping, and those who rejoice as though they were not rejoicing; buyers should conduct themselves as though they owned nothing, and those who make use of the world as though they were not using it, for the world as we know it is passing away.

I should like you to be free of all worries. The unmarried man is busy with the Lord's affairs, concerned with pleasing the Lord; but the married man is busy with this world's demands and occupied with pleasing his wife. This means he is divided. The virgin — indeed, any unmarried woman — is concerned with things of the Lord, in pursuit of holiness in body and spirit. The married woman, on the other hand, has the cares of this world to absorb her and is concerned with pleasing her husband. I am going into this with you for your own good. I have no desire to place restrictions on you, but I do want to promote what is good, what will help you to devote yourselves entirely to the Lord (1 Corinthians 7:29-35).

For too long in the Catholic Church married people have been taken as second-class citizens to the likes of priests and nuns. I thought we were over that. Now you bring on this old passage from Saint Paul again. What is going on?

Does the Catholic Church indeed demote married people to second-class citizenship? Is celibacy a higher life? This passage from First Corinthians offers a good starting point because the Church's teaching must always be measured by the Scriptures.

To understand Paul, it is necessary to enter his point of view. It can be summed up in verse 31: "The world as we know it is passing away." Eternity, or the kingdom of God, was vividly near to him. In this mind he does not sound very different from Jesus himself, who preached that the kingdom of God is in our midst.

For another thing, what Paul found most real and most important was that which lasted, which did not come to an end. In this he sounds like Jesus preaching about real life and real bread (see John 6). Everything on this earth passes away, even the greatest of gifts like marriage. Jesus also pointed out in Luke 20:35 that in heaven there will be no marriage. There we shall all be complete and self-possessed, open to intimacy with God and all others.

To get a better idea of Saint Paul's sense of urgency, let us imagine this. It is not exactly what he is saying, but it gets us close to his mind. Suppose the world were to end this evening and we knew of this. Of what concern to us would be plans to buy, to marry, to do anything? Only one thing would be, or should be, important: our relation with God and setting that right. For Saint Paul, eternity was more real than the here and now, which he knew would soon be gone.

But is it better to be a celibate? Another question, before getting to that one. Is it better to be an astronaut or a farmer? Which would you want your child to be? Astronaut — that is something great! Yes, it is. But which could we live without — astronaut or farmer? After all, we cannot eat moon rocks.

And are religious celibates (priests, Brothers, Sisters) better persons just because they are dedicated to celibacy? Of course not. And what is of greater value than being a good man, a better man, or a better woman? Is it better to be a good person or just a celibate? Do the two always go together?

About that question, whether it is better to be a celibate, it ceases to make much sense when it is brought down to daily life and real people. The ideal level is one thing, real life is another. Saint Pius X, on the day that he was consecrated a bishop, was showing his mother his bishop's ring. "Very nice," she said. "But don't forget" — and she pointed to her thin wedding band — "you wouldn't be wearing that ring unless I first wore this one!"

On the ideal level, celibacy is the higher life because it is the lifestyle of eternity. In that day everyone will be celibate. Marriage will have passed away, and all of us will live in a complete singleness open to innumerable friendships, first of all with God. In this world, however, celibacy is an unusual gift and calling, as Jesus himself said in Matthew 19:12.

On the level of real life, which life will make you a better person, a holier person? That life to which God calls you. The Scriptures teach, and the saints through the centuries insist, that what makes us holy is accepting and doing the will of God. It is not long prayers, not life in a monastery. It is wrestling with and praying through the duties and tasks of our individual lives. It is devoting ourselves to those whom God has given us and placed close to us — spouses, children, parents, friends, co-workers, parishioners.

I am no longer a virgin. I wish I were. It troubles me to think that if and when I give myself to God as a nun or to a man in marriage, I will be damaged goods.

The virginity we have been speaking of is Christian, not pagan and worldly virginity, which measures everything by physical wholeness, just as it appraises old houses and used cars. Physical experience and events cannot be undone. We all know that. Saint Thomas Aquinas does, too. Yet he points out the element that makes virginity a treasure to God — complete openness to, and emptiness for, things divine. He says this element can be restored to you. When God forgives, he *undoes* the damage we do to ourselves:

"Come now, let us set things right,
     says the LORD:
Though your sins be like scarlet,
     they may become white as snow;
Though they be crimson red,
     they may become white as wool" (Isaiah 1:18).

Jesus washes our garments white in his own blood (see Revelations 7:14).

A loving man would not be cruelly concerned about "damaged goods," but only about the same element that Saint Thomas mentioned — the openness only to him among all men. So if you marry, wear a joyful white.

I consider myself as one who loves Mary, the Mother of God. But was she really a virgin all her life, even though she was married? This I cannot understand. And it puts her at a distance from me.

The Scriptures make it clear that Jesus was born of a virgin. They say nothing after that about the married life of Mary and Joseph. Though they do mention "brothers" of Jesus, the original Greek word can also include cousins. Yet from early times the Church has honored Mary as *ever virgin,* and has designated her union with Joseph as a true marriage. Till recent times, very few people seem to have inquired into the matter. Maybe they thought it would be bad manners. But we have gotten used to snooping into what goes on behind closed doors. Another reason for our questioning is that we have come to measure so much — moral rules, for instance — by our own *experience*. What fits our experience we approve; what does not, we reject as incredible or at least improbable.

A priest was instructing a good man, well-versed in the Bible, who was interested in becoming a Catholic. The man had a question about Mary's virginal marriage because in his experience the absence of sex in a marriage meant trouble. The priest asked him to imagine himself in Joseph's place, having planned to marry a woman he loved when he found out she was carrying a child that was not his. "So in a dream God tells you that no other man gave her that child; it was God himself in his Holy Spirit. In Bethlehem she gives birth to the baby while angels sing in the sky and shepherds hasten to visit him! In another dream you are told to take your family to Egypt. But no one has told you — or your wife — how you are to live together. You can sense that she has this question, too. You have to talk.

"Now, in view of all you have seen and felt, knowing God has possessed her in an unusual way, knowing that baby is truly Someone Else, would you be able to have sex with her? Would she be able to have sex with you?"

The man paused to think, and then he said only this: "We would have to work very hard at that."

You see, there are other experiences besides ours. Maybe Mary and Joseph lived virginally because after what they had seen and known they had to live that way. After all, they were only human beings!

Well, how would this be a marriage? It would be a marriage because he would have her, and only her, to call his and count on all the days of his life. And she would have him, and only him, to be hers all the days of her life. That is the heart of marriage. Sex does not make marriage. Sex only celebrates it.

My wife has been mentally ill through many years of our married life. With medication she has been able to remain at home. I think I have been devoted, done what I ought to have done. But I feel cheated. I have only one life, one shot at happiness. I have lost out. I feel even worse for my wife.

Anyone hearing you say that has to be moved by your fidelity and sacrifice. "What would I do in his place?" We probably all ask ourselves that as we listen to you. We might also ask whether we have a practical faith in the promise we have from Jesus Christ of resurrection and eternal life. Do we really believe that there is more to life than meets the eye? But let us look to this life first, the only one we know at this point in our existence, and the one you feel the loss of.

In our griefs we can look past this life and take comfort from our faith in a life to follow. But we can also link this faith in the resurrection with an unflinching gaze upon this life, as painfully unfair as it may seem. For we believe in Jesus Christ, who before being raised to a new life suffered complete failure and a criminal's death. Had his Father played a sick joke on him? Or had he another chapter in mind for a life cut off by a most unhappy ending? Has God played a joke on you, and even more on your wife?

A very old woman was talking to a priest. Reviewing her life, as old people sometimes do, maybe as a tidying up before death, she told him about her marriage. When she was very young, she fell in love with a divorced man. The two of them wanted to marry. But her parents would not allow it. Though they came close to eloping, she broke off the relationship. She met a Catholic boy and married him. The marriage turned out miserably. She was very unhappy. To the priest it seemed that she was hardly aware of his presence as she went on. "I sometimes think I should have married that divorced man. I would have been happy. I would have been happy. No," she said, "No — *this* was my life!"

How could she say such a thing? How could she accept, peacefully accept, years of misery? Was she a philosopher? Clearly not. She believed that, as a daughter of God and a sister of Jesus Christ, God had not mocked her life. *This* was her life, and she would not change it.

Even when we look to the promise of resurrection and eternal life, we should not indulge in mere escapism. Our faith can give us nerve for this present life and courage for its hardships. Saint Paul made this wry and practical statement: "If our hopes in Christ are limited to this life only, we are the most pitiable of men" (1 Corinthians 15:19). Apparently things sometimes got that bad for him, too! But he could let himself feel that for he knew that this was the experience of only *part* of his life, even if for unbelievers it would seem like the whole of his life.

Saint Paul also said that only three things lasted — faith and hope and love — and that love was the greatest of the three. You have married in Christ. Without the grace of his sacrament, you could not have been so devoted. That devotion can never be lost to you — or to your wife. For she taught you to love by humbly looking to you for your devotion. Your marriage was a partnership of equals all along, even when she may have been reduced to childishness. Married love is held in common. She also has an unfailing treasure.

I have AIDS. I am dying. What is happening to me? Medically, I can grasp that. I meant, what is God doing to me? I know what I have done — the reason I am sick. Everybody else knows, too. Some seem happy about my illness. People never say it straight out to me, but I understand they think that God's judgment has fallen on me. I am afraid of that, too. Has God condemned me already?

You sense that God has an important part in your suffering. Right, he does. In the Bible he insists on taking final responsibility for everything that happens, whether it seems good or bad to us. But you make a mistake to conclude that you are being punished and even condemned, that God is getting even with you for flouting his moral law. We human beings get back, get even, because we can be mean. God is not like us; he is not mean. In the book of the prophet Hosea, God speaks of his sinful people as of a wayward son. Though this son deserves punishment, God says he just cannot bring himself to destroy him. And why not? "For I am God and not man" (Hosea 11:9).

But in what sense is God responsible for the bad things that happen in this world, like your illness and dying? God takes responsibility for seeing to it that evil never gets so out of hand that it destroys his loving plans for his creation.

You worry about what your illness might seem to be saying about your life and about how God sees you. Let us, however, see the sinfulness of your life — of anyone's life — in its proper setting. So often we can redefine sin as a mere frailty, a joke, or a foible that might even be somehow lovable. But the Bible sees sin above all as a malignant *power*. Your sin is the surfacing of a cancer that grips the whole world. A respected theologian defines sin this way:

> By sin we mean the sum of all the litanies of human woes, evils, and sufferings. Sin means the tragic fracturing that can happen to the human psyche as well as the tragic fracturings in the life of a nation and those superfracturings in international relationships. The litany of sin includes crimes, wars, lawsuits. . . . It includes all forms of alienation, brutality, and discrimination in our society. It also includes those more polite and subtle ways humans abuse each other. It denotes family problems, national problems, and international problems. It includes personal vices and the vices of government. Sin is contradiction; sin is violence; sin is serpentine subtlety. Sin is moral inertia; sin is inhuman response to tragic suffering.[1]

But as potent as sin might be in its viciousness and thirst to do harm, God is always more powerful. Even if we choose to let this evil genie out of the bottle, the Bible teaches that God keeps sin in check, or else the world would explode. Have you ever noticed how evil on the loose keeps going from bad to worse? The problem of pornography in our society provides an example.

The Attorney General's Commission on Pornography states that pornography increasingly focuses on sexually explicit violence. In a recent cover story on pornography, *Newsweek* magazine reflected on changes over the last fifteen years:

> The meaning of "hard core" has changed, at least in the United States. The boundaries have expanded. The term now embraces urination on children, Nazi sadomasochism and oral sex with goats. . . .
>
> "Our research shows that every time there is satiation of . . . themes, people to some degree lose their ability to be aroused" says psychologist Neil Malamuth of UCLA. "Therefore, newer themes are introduced, breaking new taboos."[2]

In other words, unless someone draws a line and holds it, evil gets crazier and crazier. Only God is strong enough to draw that line and keep it drawn. Lest the world fly to pieces, God helps us to keep sin — like the neighborhood bully — where it belongs.

You seem to realize that you have let moral evil run free in your life. Quite likely, you realized this only recently. But whatever you earlier admitted or intended, evil was slashing away at your person the whole time. Sin was killing you personally before you may have even heard of AIDS. But where does AIDS come into this? What has God to do with allowing it to strike you? It cannot be a punishment. Jesus himself ruled out the belief that physical ills are punishments for personal sins (see John 9:1-3). Could AIDS be a preventive, a check on an evil that was utterly destroying you? Yes, it could be that. But what is worse than AIDS? The loss of your soul, the second death of body and soul for all eternity. That is so hard for us to appreciate, who grow numb to sin, much as we can lie down and let ourselves fall painlessly to sleep in the snow and the killing cold. God cannot let that happen to you. You are his son, his child, and he cannot bear to lose you. He died so that you would not have to die the only real death, the second death.

When he died upon the Cross, Jesus had for company two evil men. One of them we call the Good Thief. God saw to it that the ills and evils of his life would lead him to that moment with Jesus: "Jesus, remember me when you enter upon your reign." And you know Jesus' answer: "I assure you: this day you will be with me in paradise" (Luke 23:42-43). Some say he was a thief to the end because he stole heaven. Why not do what he did?

Footnotes

1. Bernard Ramm, *Offense to Reason: The Theology of Sin* (San Francisco: Harper and Row, 1985) p. 2.
2. *Newsweek,* March 18, 1985.

A Final Word

In 1950 Pope Pius XII canonized Saint Maria Goretti, virgin and martyr. Only twelve years old, she had died on July 5, 1902, as a result of stab wounds she received while refusing to give herself up to seduction or rape.

Because Maria's father had died, her mother had to take her family to live with another family. The arrangement was rather brutal, as it must be in many modern-day tenements. Maria's mother had taken on the role of breadwinner. She worked in the fields while Maria did the housework and the cooking.

Alessandro, a young man in that other family, longed for Maria. On that July 5, while her mother worked in the fields, Alessandro cooed seduction as he had done before, and was rebuffed again. This time, however, he threatened her with a crude knife. She cried over and over, "No, it's a sin! God does not want it! You'll go to hell!" In his frustration he stabbed her repeatedly, fatally. When she was taken to the hospital and horridly operated on without anesthesia, it was clear she would die.

What for? She could have given herself up to him and no one would have blamed her. No priest would say it was any sin at all, because force and fear remove moral responsibility. What for?

Because *he* would sin, and no matter who does the sinning, sin offends God. Because she was a saint, she saw that clearly, as we do not at all. For us sin is of little consequence. We buy our way out of it cheaply, hardly thinking at all of the price Jesus paid. Why did she see things that way? Pope Pius XII recognized Maria's widsom and holiness far beyond her years. At her canonization he said:

> How great is the error of those who consider virginity an effect of the ignorance or ingeniousness of little souls without passion, without ardour, without experience, and therefore accord it only a smile of pity! How can he who has surrendered without struggle imagine what strength it requires to dominate, without a moment of weakness, the secret stirrings and urgings of the senses and of the heart, which adolescence wakens in our fallen nature to resist, without a single compromise the thousand little curiosities which impel one to see, to listen, to taste, to feel, and thus approach the lips to the intoxicating cup and inhale the deadly perfume of the flower of evil; to move through the turpitudes of the world with a firmness that is superior to all temptations, to all threats, to all seductive or mocking looks.[1]

And perhaps Maria in her innocence could not throw her body to an oppressor as we can — as though body and self become two different things. Maybe she was so "together," as we put it, that her whole body was her whole self, to be kept for God or given to a man in the sacrament of Matrimony.

Enough of "maybes." She died as she did because she loved God with her whole heart, her whole soul, her whole mind, and her whole strength. That was her rule of life, the Great Commandment. Jesus learned it as a child, lived by it, and repeated it (see Matthew 22:37). It holds for us, too. It contains a call to a passion that no human being can bear from us, even if we wanted to give it. Imagine someone saying to you that he — or she — loved you with whole heart and soul and mind and strength. If you had any sense, you would run away. You could never bear that or live up to it. The Great Commandment describes a passion all of us were created for, whether or not we ever find a great love here on earth. It is a passion for God, who made us to love him even when earth and marriage are no more. Saint Augustine expressed the truth unforgettably: ''You have made us for yourself, O Lord, and our hearts are restless until they rest in you.''

We might say, then, that Maria Goretti had no choice. Her sanctity was her destiny. Ours is, too, but we fail to see the sense of this. We will someday. But for now we puzzle over what the Catholic Church preaches and commands, even though she knows that only saints can really understand. But she knows, too, that God has called all of us to be saints. If he does not have his way with us in this life, well, then he has a mysterious space after death, where in his love he purifies our desire so that it longs only for what lasts eternally — God himself and all good things in him.

Just before she died, Maria was to be given Holy Communion. Because she was so weak and tired, she was asked whether she knew what she was about to receive. ''Yes,'' she said, ''it is Jesus, whom I shall soon see in heaven.'' Everything else was passing away; nothing else mattered. So it will be one day for each of us. May we, too, see Jesus in heaven. Amen.

Footnotes

1. C. E. Maguire, *Maria Goretti, Martyr of Purity* (New York: Catholic Book Publishing Co., 1950), pp. 8-9.

OTHER BOOKS ON MORALITY

FOLLOWING CHRIST: A Handbook of Catholic Moral Teaching
by Daniel L. Lowery, C.SS.R.

A simple, straightforward book that answers the most-often-asked questions about morality and offers moral guidelines for living in today's world. **$3.50**

WHAT'S RIGHT? A Teenager's Guide to Christian Living
by Jim Auer

Through this book, young people will learn the lowdown on high-priority topics like "The Meaning of Life," "Sexuality," and "Integrity." It explains that morality is more than a list of "don'ts" designed to keep people from having a good time. **$3.95**

SIN: A Christian View for Today
by Xavier Thevenot

Is original sin an outdated idea? What's the difference between sin and feeling guilty? This book explores these and other questions to help Christians better understand the influence of sin in their personal lives. **$2.95**

IS LOVE IN AND SIN OUT? A Look at Basic Morality
by Russell M. Abata, C.SS.R., S.T.D.

Written to help questioning minds find some straight answers in areas of right and wrong, this book offers practical guidelines for daily living, using real life examples and questions for reflection. **$2.95**

THE TEN COMMANDMENTS AND TODAY'S CHRISTIAN
by Finbarr Connolly, C.SS.R., and Peter Burns, C.SS.R.

This brief book offers readers a basic understanding of the Ten Commandments as they apply to the world today. Each commandment is discussed in terms of its Old Testament context, its inherent "core value," and its application to everyday life. **$1.50**

Order from your local bookstore or write to:
Liguori Publications, Box 060, Liguori, Missouri 63057
*(Please add 75¢ for postage and handling for
first item ordered and 25¢ for each additional item.)*